BEYOND
MAGENTA

BEYOND MAGENTA

Transgender Teens Speak Out

SUSAN KUKLIN

CANDLEWICK PRESS

First edition 2014

Library of Congress Catalog Card Number pending
ISBN 978-0-7636-5611-9

13 14 15 16 17 18 TTP 10 9 8 7 6 5 4 3 2 1

Printed in Huizhou, Guangdong, China

This book was typeset in Mendoza.

Candlewick Press
99 Dover Street
Somerville, Massachusetts 02144

visit us at www.candlewick.com

For Bailey with love

CONTENTS

NOTES AND RESOURCES 163

A NOTE TO THE READER

The stories you are about to read are of real people, members of the transgender community, whom I have come to appreciate and respect. An author is supposed to be objective, and this author has withheld judgment while conducting interviews, taking photographs, and writing. But my subjects' willingness to brave bullying and condemnation in order to reveal their individual selves makes it impossible to be nothing less than awestruck.

As part of their transition, most of the participants have changed their birth names. Whenever I refer to them, I use their chosen name and PGPs — preferred gender pronouns — before, during, and after their transition. My comments are represented in a different typeface.

Since each chapter is different, like a series of short stories, you can read them as I placed them or in whatever order you want.

Susan Kuklin

SPECTRUM

JESSY

The House of My Soul

When Jessy got his period, he was confused. He says, "It was, like, 'Oh-my-good-ness!' I cried to my mom: 'Why, why, why? Why am I a woman? I don't want this. I don't want to give birth to a child. I want kids, but I don't want to be the one giving birth. I don't need menstruation. Mom, I don't want this.'

"'You think I want it?' she said. 'Every woman deals with it. It's what makes you a woman.'

"And I was, like, 'Oh, God! Here we go.'"

I was never a person who said, "I hate my body." I just wanted it to fit more with what I felt inside. I ate right and treated my body with care because it's the house of my soul. I've always loved my body, and now I love it even more because it fits how I feel.

I've never been gay-bashed. No one has ever said really hurtful things to me. I've never experienced much disrespect from my peers. I think that's because I have a positive attitude. I've always been happy and bubbly, and I've never made people feel uncomfortable about who I am. My Facebook page says "male — so happy I'm taking T," so I'm out there. ("T" stands for *testosterone,* a male hormone.)

All in all, I had a fun childhood. I did a lot. I took music lessons — piano and guitar. I was in honors band, and I also played the saxophone. Everyone has bad times, sad times, and I have too, but mostly I'm the funny, loud, happy person in the room. I'm the one making jokes, playing pranks. Ask my advisor. Ask my friends.

My real name is Kamolchanok. It's a long name. I'm Thai. I'm from Bangkok. When I moved to the U.S. with my parents, they said, "No one's ever going to say your name properly, so let's just call you Jessica." I was okay with that when I was little.

I was always a tomboy, always the girl who played with boys. After a while, people said, "We're going to call you Jess. Jessy." I still use my real name on legal documents, but everybody knows me as Jessy.

I'm an only child, an only daughter. My parents call me their son now.

In the beginning . . .

All the Girls Wore Dresses

When I was three or four, my parents moved us to the U.S. because of my dad's career. He's a diplomat. We lived in Cooper City, Florida, until I was about thirteen.

As a three-year-old, I had a lot of boy friends and we were always playing with toy guns. One day I went into the boys' bathroom with them, and my mom pulled me out. "You can't go into that bathroom." I was heartbroken.

"Why can't I go into that bathroom?"

"You're a girl — you have to act like one. You can't always be with the boys." From that early age, I knew that being a girl is not me — that is not how I feel.

I have preschool pictures of me wearing a suit and a necktie. It was at a Valentine's Day party at school, and you had to dress nice. All the girls at school wore dresses. I said, "Dad, I don't want to wear a dress. Can you pick out a suit and a necktie for me?" And my dad bought a boy's suit and a clip-on necktie. I was about six. I loved wearing suits and neckties. It felt right to me. But usually I wore dresses and stuff.

In first or second grade, I had a little crush on a girl. I remember thinking, *Oh, she's so pretty.* I wanted to pull her hair, to bother her. *Should I be feeling this way?* I wondered if the other girls felt this way.

When I was eight, I started taking karate and boxing. I remember how much I liked punching the heck out of the boys; I never wanted to fight little girls. It felt weird. I knew I was better than the girls, and I wanted more of a challenge. One time, even though we wore foam masks, I got a cut on my face. My dad saw it. "Oh, I don't like to see you get punched," he said, and made me stop.

Instead, my mom forced me to take dancing. "Try it! If you don't like it, we'll change." She wanted me to try Thai dancing, but because of playing basketball and soccer at a really young age, my hands were not flexible. I had no flexibility in my body. I couldn't even bend over to touch the tip of my toes.

She made me do a little tap, jazz dancing, and ballet. I cried every time I had to go. "Nooooo!" I would hold on to the bar and literally cry my eyes out. "I don't want to wear spandex! *No!*" I just cried. When it came time for the recital, she begged me, "Please, just do it. I promise I will never make you do it again. Just do the recital." I did it. I felt like crap! I wore a sexy little red dress and bows in my hair, and I had to pose. I just wanted to cry. "Why are you making me do this?" I was so mad.

After that I started playing little-league soccer and was the star player. Everybody said, "Your daughter's amazing." All the coaches wanted me on their team.

Soccer and basketball were my main games because my dad loves those sports. He would teach me how to kick, how to shoot. He bought me a big hoop, and I would play with all the boys.

Puberty's Reality

Once Jessy started puberty, reality came crashing down. There was one thing he did not want.

Breasts! I was starting to develop breasts. Oh, crap. I hated bras, never liked wearing them. I had always been a sports-bra person.

It wasn't just looks. It's the way people treated girls. I can hold my own door, thank you. I can protect myself.

When Jessy turned twelve, his family returned to Thailand. He learned to read and write Thai fluently at an international school that used an American curriculum. The textbooks were from America, and the teachers were mostly teaching in English. This helped him feel comfortable as a Thai and as an American. But yet something was wrong, and he couldn't put his finger on it.

In Thailand, they call people like me "tomboy," which is basically a butch lesbian. I guess people had questions about me. I was questioning me too. I wasn't sure what I was, so I tried to make people think I was straight. I tried to be a big girly-girl, just to fit in. No matter how pretty I looked, I felt uncomfortable. I felt like I wasn't right in a physical sense.

I went on a date or two with boys from my school—my mom even met them—but it was never an intimate relationship. It was, like, "I really like you as a friend, you're an awesome guy, and I want to hang out with you, but I don't want to go beyond that level." It felt so uncomfortable.

I had a problem with the clique of girls I was in. They were the prettiest girls in school, the conceited clique.

"We're the prettiest! We're the most popular," Jessy says, using a singsong voice, raising his eyebrows, and shaking his head from side to side in amused disgust.

They tried to push me. "You should wear this. You should wear that!" It wasn't me.

When I was with them, I'd say, "Oh, I think he's so cute!" But what I really thought was, *Oh my God, what am I saying? I think* she's *so cute!*

I had long hair and was trying hard to act like a girl. When I told them I wanted to cut my hair, they wanted to know why.

"Wait, you're not my mom," I said. "Why are you asking me this?"

At one point, they asked, "Are you gay?" I said I didn't know, and they started saying things that were kind of mean. No, not kind of—it was mean.

"I can't believe you are that kind of person," my *close* friend said, glaring at me like I was from another planet.

"Why would you do that?"

"Tell me if you are!"

I said, "You say you're my friend. Why can't you accept me for who I am? How can you say those things to me?"

How could I call these people my closest friends when they didn't even know who I was? That's not the definition of friend. A friend is someone you can share things with. You can be yourself around. If you had a crush on someone, you can tell your friend. I could not do that with those girls.

Finally, I said good-bye to that clique, and I ate lunch alone. I was hurt. I was kind of lonely. But I was not going to finish high school there, anyway — I was going to the States, so whatever . . .

When Jessy was known as Jessica

During that time I thought, *Am I really a lesbian?* I was scared and unsure about myself. Before I came out, I had to make sure that this was what I wanted for myself. That this was who I wanted to be.

By ninth grade, I really got into sports. I played basketball at the time, on the girls' varsity team. I tried to dress pretty, but I felt so out of place in a skirt. Every time I looked in the mirror, I felt I shouldn't be wearing it. I'm *not* ladylike. That's not me.

Now, when I show people a picture of me as a girl, no one believes me. In the picture, I was wearing lipstick and a dress. Everyone says, "That's your sister."

"No, I swear to God it's me."

During Jessy's early high-school years, he didn't know what the word transgender *meant. He was only questioning his sexual orientation. He thought,* Hey, if you like women and you're a woman, then you're a lesbian. *He didn't know about gender diversity because he was young.*

7

On the one hand, he wanted to please his family and be accepted by society. On the other hand, he knew something was not right.

At first I thought maybe there is something psychologically wrong with me because I was thinking this way, because I was feeling this way. Am I abnormal? I was a little insecure. I didn't have anyone to talk to. I had to work through it on my own.

I asked myself, *Well, what's wrong with liking the same sex? Is it sinful? Why does society view it as something so bad, so taboo?* Love is love, and whoever you feel you love, express it, it's okay. It's not like I'm a crook or a robber or doing harmful things to people. I'm just trying to be who I am. I'm just trying to give the love that I have to someone who happens to be the same sex as me. I didn't see anything wrong with that. I started questioning a lot of things about society—especially social roles.

Time passes. . . .

Coming Out, Part One

Tenth grade was when a lot of drama happened in my life. I was, like, *enough!* No more! I was tired of trying to make other people happy around me. *I was tired!* I could be so much more if I could just be myself.

I started to hang out with a group of girls who were open lesbians. I cut my hair to my earlobes and spiked it up. Spiky. I got into my new look. I started dating girls and I started to become the real me. And that's the year when my relationship with my mom got a little rocky.

When I first came out to my mom as a lesbian, she withdrew. She had to step back, like, Whoa. A lot of this was happening because of puberty. I wanted to go out; I wanted to do this and that. I was exploring myself. Those were my watershed years, years when every kid, straight or not, rebels and thinks their parents don't know anything. Everything they said was outdated. Coming out made things even more complicated.

The thing was, although I dated lesbians, I was attracted to straight women. I was attracted to girls who like men. The girl I started dating was straight. Her sister was a lesbian, but she herself was straight. I guess she was going through what I would call an experimental phase. I had classes with her every day, so we saw each other all the time. We became close, and things easily elevated. But if she had just seen me on the street or something, I don't think she would have liked me.

I wore retro-looking suits with slim neckties or bow ties. I was almost like a metrosexual man; I liked getting my nails done. A metrosexual is a guy who has certain female qualities. He likes being pampered. Hair. Nails. He dresses sophisticated. He's always on point with his style. The shoes have to match the shirt. That's something girls do. But metrosexual men are into that as well.

Back in the Closet

After finishing tenth grade in Thailand, Jessy moved back to Florida. His parents wanted him to go to college in the States and thought it would be easier to get in if he went to high school here too. Since his parents were living in Thailand, Jessy stayed with an uncle. Although Miami is a liberal area, Jessy went to a strict, Christian, coed high school.

My life became harder. I didn't want people talking about me. I didn't want them on my back. I had heard that there were a few lesbians at the school who had posted pictures of themselves and their partners on Facebook or MySpace. Some school administrator found out, printed the pictures, and showed them to the principal. They were almost suspended. That basically shoved me back into the closet.

I grew my hair out and looked more feminine. I didn't tell anybody that I was attracted to women. I said to myself that I'm here to get good grades and finish high school. I don't need to share my sexual identity with people. I made a lot of close friends, but they didn't know about me.

At the school, everybody loved Jessy. He was smart and funny and very popular. He was a terrific basketball player. But there was always a wall. That's because Jessy was living a lie. He told no one, not even his closest friends, who he really was.

• • •

High-school graduation

When I was sixteen, I saw a TV episode about the transgender community, and the first thing that came into my head was "*Oh, my god! That could definitely be me!*"

I was starting to come to terms with my sexual orientation. I wanted to be the masculine figure in a relationship with a woman, to be seen as a straight man attracted to women.

I wanted to transition, but before I did, my mother had to be the first to know because we have always been so close. I knew that I could not go into transition without her knowing about it. I would never do that. Still, I kept these thoughts to myself, never saying anything till the summer before my last year in high school.

Coming Out, Part Two

Back in Florida, I started dating a girl I met on a social networking site. We had a relationship, but it didn't last that long — it was more like a fling. But because of her, it became important for me to tell my friends that I was in a relationship with a girl. Before starting college, I wanted to make it clear to my friends in high school that I date girls; I wasn't attracted to men. I called myself a butch lesbian.

On the day I graduated, I came out to my friends. I said, "There's something I have to tell you guys. I'm dating a girl."

They said, "Yeah, we kind a figured that because you're not the most feminine person. We sensed it, but we didn't want to ask you. We respected your privacy. We didn't want to make you feel uncomfortable. But we feel bad that you couldn't tell us because you're our friend, and we love you no matter what." It was a good way to leave high school.

It was also a good way to start college, knowing that my friends in high school accepted me as I am. When I went back to see them spring break of freshman year, it was so different because by then I was a hundred percent me. It was beautiful.

Coming Out Trans — to Mom

By this time, Jessy's parents had moved to Nairobi because his dad had become the minister counselor for the Thai embassy in Kenya. Jessy, who wants to become a doctor, spent the summer with them while participating in a medical internship.

I said, "Mom, I've been reading a lot about the transgender community. I've been reading a lot about taking testosterone. I think that's what I will be doing once I start my sophomore year in college. At the end of summer, I'm going to find a place where I can begin transitioning." I said it to her just that way.

I could tell she was a little bit disappointed, not disappointed but drawn back. Actually, she was kind of shocked, shaking her head, like, Why would you do this? "Why would you want to?" she asked. "Why can't you be comfortable with yourself? I don't see other lesbians doing this."

I explained that I never felt like a lesbian. I never wanted to look feminine. I'm attracted to the whole feminine look, but I never wanted it for myself. I love long hair. I love dresses. But I never wanted that on me; I wanted that on another person, the person that I was attracted to. "Besides, just because someone else doesn't do it doesn't mean I can't do it."

I told my mom that I wanted people to see me as a man in a heterosexual relationship. I wanted to be referred to as *he*. I wanted to live my life as the man of the house, masculine. I know there are butch lesbians, and all that stuff, but I didn't want to be that. I just wanted to be a normal man.

She took it in. She cried about it. She cried in front of me about it. Honestly, it made me feel awful. It made me feel I was doing something horribly wrong. I felt like a screw-up. But I'm not a screw-up. I told myself that sooner or later she was going to come to terms with this. I told myself that as with everything in life, things happen for a reason.

Once she cried, I took a step back. For a while, I said nothing more about it. After all, I had to understand where she was coming from. I had to give her time to come to terms with me. As a new parent in the delivery room, when the doctor says you have a girl, you expect to have a daughter. You expect your child is going to be what society has paved for her. So I realized that I had to give her time.

. . .

Two or three weeks later, I talked to my mom again. I told her, "I want to transition. I'm at a point where I'm responsible enough to carry on my transition."

She said, "I don't know. I can't accept this yet. You're my daughter, and I want you to be the way you are. I'm happy with you being a lesbian; don't transition. Don't physically change yourself."

We got into a heated argument about it. "Mom, I do everything to make you proud. I'm the child who never disappoints you. This is the only time I'm asking you to understand something about me. I know it's hard. I don't expect you to completely understand me, but please try." I said this over and over and over until she finally accepted it. That truly showed her unconditional love.

Open communication is beautiful. Now she's completely fine with having a son. She even put me down as her son on Facebook. Recently, she told me, "You know, I think you're going to be a very handsome man."

It's a process. It's a gradual process.

My mom's my best friend and I talk to her about everything. It's always been that way, but now it's even stronger because she's proven to me that she accepts me for who I am, not what I am.

I said to her, "Mom, I was always the kid who wanted the highest grade in class. I was the girl who beat the boys in basketball. I tried to be the best in everything, just 'cause I wanted people to see beyond my exterior look. I want people to see my accomplishments and say, 'Wow.'"

My mom said, "I want you to blow the world away with your transition as a man. Start working out. Go to the gym. Look good. And you can't be a fat man. No girl likes that."

I love my mom. Without her support I probably wouldn't be as open about my experience transitioning.

To Dad

I don't think my mother told my dad about me wanting to transition. He knew I was butch lesbian and that I was dating girls because I was bringing girls to the house back in Thailand. But he didn't know about me wanting to transition.

A very close family friend has a nephew who was a trans woman, and my dad told me about her. I said, "Well what if I go through that one day?"

"I don't want much from you. I just want you to be happy and successful. I want you to be happy who you are. I want to see you become a good person, someone with values and someone with morals. That's all I expect of you. I don't care what else you do. And I want you to take care of us when we're older."

My dad has always been a very busy man, so I've not spent as much time with him as I would have wanted. He was always traveling, always on the go. My mom raised me. My dad was the disciplinarian. He's a strict and stern man. He'll say something once, and if you don't get it, you're going to be disciplined.

He's also very intelligent. He loves reading. He loves to study. He loves to build things. Everything I've learned as a man comes from my father. Be strong. Don't cry. Don't whine.

My mom is more nurturing. She's the softer side of me. She's the one who made me a hopeless romantic. She taught me how to make something look aesthetic and beautiful. She showed me that it's okay to be emotional, to be sweet, to be caring, to be gentle.

She taught me how to cook because every girl wants a guy who can cook. She taught me how to clean so that there's not a speck of dust in the house. That's my mom. She's a very caring, sweet, loving person.

Almost up-to-date . . .

LGBTQ

I'm a college student now. Saint Joseph's College is a private school with a Catholic name. I'm on a full scholarship, and I try to be a leader in school activities. I work for the campus activities board. It's a very honorable position, and I like the jobs that I do. I ran for vice president of the school. I'm on the school newspaper. I know everybody at the school, and everybody knows me.

Years ago there used to be an LGBTQ (Lesbian, Gay, Bi, Trans, Queer) group, but it died out. As the only transgender student, I brought a new kind of diversity to the school. I became the president of the new LGBTQ.

The president of the college said that what I was doing was great, and that the whole school supported me.

Transitioning

Jessy went online to research transgender forums. The Callen-Lorde Community Health Center, in Manhattan, has a program called HOTT, Health Outreach to Teens, which helps transgender teenagers transition. Jessy went to the clinic, ready to take the necessary steps to transition to male.

Not so fast. Before Jessy could begin the physical process of transitioning, he had to go through sixteen sessions of therapy. Sixteen? That would mean waiting four months. He wanted the hormone shots now. Not now, yesterday!

The therapist, Nicole Davis, explained that before he transitioned, he had to be sure that this was what he wanted to do. It's a matter of discovery, of self-exploration. As a trans male, Jessy will need hormone shots, testosterone, for the rest of his life. That's a big step.

Nicole was amazing! I love her! I was very comfortable with her from the start. I'm so glad I had those sixteen sessions with her. It gave me the time to make sure transition was what I wanted, and to make sure I was ready to deal with certain obstacles that come with transition. Like, when to start using the men's bathroom, how to switch pronouns, and how to interact with my family and friends as a different sex.

Nicole provided the information so that I could formulate my own decision. She never said, "Oh, you can do it." She would listen to what I had to say, and ask, "What do you really want to do? Is that how you feel?" She helped me come to my own decisions. She gave me space to think through things on my own, which really helped, because I was going through such a confusing time. Basically I needed someone to shut up and listen to me. And Nicole did that very well.

I had periods of doubt. At one point, I thought maybe I shouldn't take the hormones. Maybe I should just stay like this. I love being healthy and was scared about possible risks.

At night, before I'd fall asleep, I would lie awake in the dark, under the covers, tossing and turning, thinking. In the daytime, I'd daydream. I was afraid that there would be technical difficulties.

How would I be seen in the workplace? On official papers I'd be identified as female. In person I'd appear male. How would an employer react?

There were sporadic moments when I said to myself, "All right, I'm ready! I'm completely ready!" Then, spontaneously, I'd go, "Oh, my God, wait!"

I want to be a doctor for the transgender community. I want to be able to say to someone, "I'll do your surgery for free." For someone like me, feeling good about the way you look is so important. It adds to your self-esteem. It defines how you function in everyday life. If you look in the mirror every day and say, "I don't want to look like this," you won't have the will, the drive, to be anything in life.

I would take one step forward, then one step back. I was like a little kid about to jump in the water. My toes were in the water and I'm about to jump in, but then I'd pull my toes out 'cause it would be too cold.

I also didn't want the dependence of taking hormones every two weeks to stop me from doing other things in life. I love to travel, and I see myself working in third-world countries. What if I got a job somewhere but I couldn't go because I had to be in a place where I could get hormones. What would I do?

Jessy talked about these concerns with Nicole. She helped him understand that there's always a way around things if you want it badly enough. People would hire Jessy because of his skills, not because of his gender. Bottom line: Was Jessy ready to change? Midway through the therapy sessions, he decided that he was ready.

Then he thought of yet another obstacle.

Jessy is a Thai citizen, using a Thai passport. He's in the States on a student visa. In Thailand, you cannot change your legal gender.

He worried what would happen when he went through customs looking male with a passport that said he was female. Jessy gave this as a reason not to take the hormones. It was just too risky.

Nicole told him that taking hormones was his choice, and his choice alone, but that he would be able to change his passport picture, and the clinic could write a letter explaining that he's transitioning, so he wouldn't have a hard time passing through customs.

Finally, after thinking and talking and weighing his options, Jessy said to Nicole, "You know what? I'm ready! I want to transition. This is me! The world will have to just deal with it."

In March 2011, I started taking testosterone injections. After being on them one month, my metabolism was crazy. I started noticing more underarm hair, and my muscle mass was increasing a little. People noticed the changes. Even Nicole said I looked a little bit different.

I ate constantly. All I thought about was food. I ate two bowls of spaghetti when before I only ate one. And on top of that, I found myself eating two scoops of ice cream. I overdosed on tortilla chips and salsa. At night, I could have sworn I'd eaten an hour ago, but I would be hungry, like I hadn't eaten for four hours. Food. Food. Food. I just wanted to eat! Most of my budget went to my stomach.

My sleeping habits changed too. I wanted to sleep more. That's how it is for biological men too. They sleep longer than women.

Maybe because I'm young, my body took in the hormones very fast. I got the shots every two weeks. For the first two shots, I had a half dose. That's the protocol. After the first two shots, you can decide if you want to keep to that amount or increase it to a full dose. How fast you want to transition is your personal choice.

At first I thought I would not rush it. I would just do low doses of T and change slowly. But then, once I started to feel the changes and I started to see myself looking how I really, truly wanted to look, I got so excited. I wanted the full dose.

In the beginning, I told my friends that I was transitioning and they were, like, "Okay, what does that mean?"

TRANSITIONING

Left: Photograph taken April 6

Right: Photograph taken April 18

Below: Photograph taken May 5

"It doesn't mean anything," I said, "but it would be more appropriate to call me *he,* instead of *she,* because it would match what I identify myself as and what I look like from the outside."

They were completely cool and honest when they told me, "Okay, you're our friend, and we respect you. But you're going to have to give us time. We've always called you *she,* and now you want us to switch in a night. That can't happen so fast."

I saw that they tried; they really did try. Sometimes they'd slip, call me *she,* and go, "Oh, *oh,* oh, oh," and get right back to *he* and *him.*

Girls started talking to me differently. "Hey, you're looking more like a guy every day," they told me. My best friend, who's female, said that she couldn't wait to hear me with a deeper voice. Me too.

Most of my guy friends were happy I'm taking T. We worked out together. We had a brotherly bond. The frat guys wanted me to pledge. We went on guy nights where we talked about girl problems. It was very natural to talk about girls. The friends that I had, the community that I made at school, were very open.

Women's Lockers, Men's Bathroom

I was still going to the women's lockers. Then I thought, *Wait! I'm getting further and further into my therapy, and sooner or later, I'm going to sound like, and completely look like, a man. So how do I handle the gym?* I was close with the gym owner, so I planned to tell him, "If you start seeing me going to the men's locker room, it's because I've transitioned to male."

I won't use the shower, though, since the bottom part of me hasn't changed. In general I hate using public showers. I prefer to shower at home.

Ever since I started transitioning, I've used a stall in the men's room. When you see me you say, "That's a male." It would be awkward if I used a women's bathroom. A lot of men are pee shy; they use the stalls, not the urinals. Women are different. When women go in the bathroom, they look around, talk, they put on makeup. But men just go in, do their business, and leave. They're not looking to chat or get friendly, so they don't really care whether you use a urinal or not. I think men are less complicated.

Prince Charming

Back in Thailand, I had some friends and family who knew about my transition. They called me "Prince Charming." They sent me Facebook messages, like, "Prince Charming, how are you? You look handsome." I had that support 'cause my mom proudly told people about me.

I recently went back and the neighbors said, "You don't look close to being a female anymore."

"Yeah." What can I say?

"You look really good, though."

"Thank you."

At the end of Jessy's sophomore year, he returned to Thailand to do a biomedical internship at the Chulabhorn Research Institute, in Bangkok. Before he left New York, a nurse taught him how to self-inject the hormones so that he could be independent.

For a split second I thought, *Oh, my God, I'm giving myself a shot.* I had a two-second adrenaline rush. I wasn't scared, but I was anxious and had a kinda jittery feeling.

Now I inject myself in the thigh every two weeks. My thigh gets really sore, but the shot itself doesn't hurt. It's just a little tiny pinch. But it makes my thigh so sore, I feel like I've run five miles on the treadmill. The first time I did it, I couldn't move my leg when I went to bed. Ouch. Ouch. Now it's, like, I'm running, jumping, skipping.

Three months later . . .

I pass one hundred percent as male now. Everything about me is very masculine: my voice, my facial hair; even my skin texture is thicker, rougher. I'm a lot more muscular. I was never able to do pull-ups; I had poor upper body strength. Now pull-ups are so easy. I have a lot more stamina, endurance. I lift things now and don't get tired. So there's definitely been a change.

Luckily, the women in my family don't have large breasts, so I assumed that I wouldn't, either. And now the testosterone in my body reduces the fat in my breasts.

Photograph taken September 16

Usually, though, I bind. A binder is a double layer of spandex that looks like a tank top. It's very tight so when you pull it over you it compresses your chest. Binding, honestly, is very uncomfortable. Binding makes it hard to breathe.

Now that I'm going through transition, I've finally escaped. It's wonderful. I'm going through puberty all over again, and I'm excited. When I look in the mirror, it's like, "Oh, I'm hitting the puberty that I *wanted,* not the other one." If I see a pimple, I go, "Okay, I'm becoming a guy. Yeah. Look at that! Look at that!"

Before my transition, I was so frustrated because I really wanted to look muscular. Although I worked out, I could never get the body I wanted. As a woman I had estrogen, and estrogen produces fat instead of muscle. It pained me so much to see my male friends at the gym, friends I grew up with. I watched them go through puberty and was so jealous. They had the bodies I wanted. It didn't make me mad, but it made me a little bit sad. Guys have more upper-body strength. They are physically stronger because they have testosterone, not estrogen. Every time I saw a guy working out, I thought, *I want that body! I want to be able to do that!*

I took a sociology class where we discussed male and female gender roles. Believe it or not, people have this assumption that females are supposed to take up less space than males. When I'm on the subway and I sit with my legs spread out, people respect my space. Before, when I was still seen as female, people would sit down and squish me.

I take on the male social role now. I've always wanted to be treated that way, so it's not a problem, but it took some getting used to. When I go places, like to a restaurant, the waiter flat out calls me "sir." Before it was, like, "Mister?" "Miss?" People were hesitant to come up to me. "Is that a guy or a girl?"

Now 99.5 percent of people call me "sir" wherever I go. When I'm walking with my girlfriend, they respect me more because they see me as a guy with his gal. They don't hassle us.

Whoa, back up. Girlfriend? Jessy breaks into a big smile and continues his train of thought.

Before, the guys on the street wouldn't respect two women together. But now that they see me as a man, they back off. Even when I go to a club with my girlfriend, guys don't mess with us. One guy tried to go up to my girlfriend and I was, like, "Excuse me," and he's, like, "Sorry, man." And he just backed off.

Transformation

Because Jessy now has a partner, our one-on-one interview changes to a dialogue. Her name is Nan. They met at a gym in Jessy's second week in Bangkok. He immediately asked her out. She immediately turned him down flat.

"I feel nervous for love," Nan says six months later, sipping red wine in my studio.

JESSY: She was not open. She had her guard up. She gave me her office number. Her *office* number? Obviously she didn't want to go out with me.

A month later, we happened to be working out at the same time. I went up to her and asked if she remembered me. She didn't, actually, but she pretended that she did. I ended up calling her office number a day later, supposedly to ask her something work related.

Nan was a part-time model working for a fitness company that distributes vitamin supplements. Jessy saw a way in: "Hey, do you sell L-Carnitine?" Nan told him that her company did sell it and that they would give him an employee discount if he picked it up at the office.

JESSY: At the end of the workday, I went to her office to pick up the supplement. "Did you eat yet?" I asked her.

NAN: "No, I'm not hungry."

JESSY: "Can you get a cup of coffee with me?"

NAN: "No."

Photograph taken December 19

NAN: The main reasons I did not accept his invitation were because he was much younger than I was and because I only dated older women. Never men! A third reason I wasn't interested was because he lived in New York.

Jessy literally begged her to have a cup of coffee. Nan remembers saying, "Why should I give you a chance? What makes you think you're on my level?"

JESSY: I said to her, "Give me two weeks. I'm not asking you to love me. I'm not asking you to sleep with me. I'm just asking you for a little bit of your time before you jump and make assumptions."

Nan finally gave in and went to Starbucks for a quick cup of coffee. They ended up talking there for hours. A week later, she accepted his invitation to dinner. She gave him a chance and was not disappointed.

JESSY: On our first date, I told her I liked her. And I told her I was transgender. I didn't want to keep anything from her. If I wanted her to like me for who I am, she needed to know about the things that make me who I am. I didn't rush Nan. I didn't call every day.

Although Nan accepted Jessy's transition, she never uses the pronoun he. She only refers to him as she. Surprisingly, Jessy, who spent years convincing his family and friends to use male pronouns, doesn't mind.

NAN: I was attracted to Jessy because of her optimistic, sunny personality, not because of her gender. Definitely not her gender! I responded to the feminine features that still remained, including her soft skin. But I didn't like the fact that she was taking male hormones. I said to her, "Why? Why are you taking your hormones and things? I like soft skin. I like everything woman."

JESSY: I guess she came to terms with it. I've been able to show her that my gender doesn't affect how much I love her. I explained that I wasn't going to get any hairier than this. I'm Thai. In general, Asian guys don't have much hair. I'm not going to get a huge beard; this is the most I'll get.

I think she's okay with it now. We openly talk about it, and we share how we feel about it. That makes me really love her, because she tries to understand me. This is the first relationship where I can be truly open about everything. I don't have any secrets. I'm not scared to share my past with her. I'm not scared to share things about my family, things that I've been through. She's the first person I've completely opened up to.

I really don't care about pronouns anymore. A pronoun doesn't define who I am. I have a male role in society. I'm proud to be transgender. It's an enriching experience and a big part of my life. But yet I can't get rid of the fact that I was born a biological female. I've had the privilege of being born into a female body and living in a masculine body. I like the fact that I've changed my sex.

God made me transgender for a reason. Maybe not God, but whoever created me. Whoever created me made me this way for a reason. I enjoy life from a different perspective. I can see the world simultaneously from a male and a female perspective. When I speak with Nan, I understand where she's coming from as a woman. I understand the days when Nan has her period. I understand the days when she's cranky 'cause I know what all of that is like. And then, when I speak to my male friends, I get along with all the guys 'cause I think like a guy. I always thought like a guy. I had a guy attitude.

Physiologically Jessy is male because his body operates on testosterone. But biologically, he's still female. He will always have XX chromosomes. Men are born with XY chromosomes and women are born XX. You cannot change your genetic makeup. Everybody is born with male and female hormones, estrogen and testosterone. When a person hits puberty, males have a surge of testosterone and very little estrogen. Females have a surge of estrogen and very little testosterone. Testosterone activates certain genes, like those causing facial hair. Women also have facial hair, but because they have very little testosterone, it's not apparent.

JESSY: I still have a feminine side. As I said before, I'm more like a metrosexual man. I like getting my nails done. I admit that. I like going to a spa and having my nails—*not* colored! No! Not colored, buffed.

NAN: I was surprised how much attention Jessy pays to her appearance. "What? You take care of yourself? Your face? Your hair? Your body?"

JESSY: I want to be good-looking for her.

Jessy smiles broadly while stroking Nan's arm.

The thing is, she's always dated masculine girls; she never dated feminine lesbians. And most of them, she told me, didn't really take care of themselves. She's always had to dress them up, pretty them up. This is the first time there is someone in her life that can take care of himself. I go to the gym. I exercise. I eat healthy—I try to eat healthy. I take care of my skin, my hair. She's surprised. She's never met someone like me. She's getting used to me.

NAN [grinning at Jessy]: She's almost like a gay man.

JESSY: I've been taught that your body houses your soul. For you to be emotionally happy, you need to be physically happy; you need to be in good health. So I've always had this concept of taking care of myself.

Nan has been in New York only a few weeks. She's here on a visitor's visa. Is she adjusting? "It takes time," she says almost in a whisper. Jessy is helping her adjust. It's not easy because the culture here is so different.

JESSY: A few days ago, Nan was walking down the street and a few men hollered, 'Yo, what's up?' She got really scared. I said, "You're in Brooklyn! That's normal."

Jessy is changing too. He no longer binds his chest. Now that testosterone is taking effect, his chest size has gone down.

JESSY: And because I work out a lot, my chest is almost turning into muscle. Aren't my arms nice?

NAN [whispering]: Yes.

JESSY [laughing, totally enjoying Nan's comments]: Nan's very confused. She likes a masculine figure but maybe not the sexual part of it. She's not sexually attracted to men, but she likes a masculine figure—not over-masculine, like muscles the size of her head. But she likes someone toned, with a nice physique.

NAN: At first she surprised me. I had never been with anyone like her—her body, her legs, and arms.

Before meeting Jessy, I dated butch lesbians, known as "tom" lesbians, tomboys, in Thailand. Although they dressed like guys, none of them were on testosterone. Unlike Jessy, they still had feminine features, such as high voices. Jessy's voice has become deeper now that she's taking hormone shots.

JESSY: We've had a lot of culture clashes. Even though I'm Thai, I have American values. I've mostly lived an American lifestyle. Sometimes, during our meals together, she tries to feed me. Are you kidding me? I was, like, "What are you doing? American women don't do that."

NAN: I was just trying to take care of her, like we do in Thailand.

JESSY: She'd feed me and she'd fold my clothes. Folding? I can fold my own clothes. Nan was hurt. She couldn't understand why I did not accept the things she wanted to do for me. I wasn't trying to hurt her; I'm just not used to that. I hadn't been exposed to it. It was all so new.

Sure, my mother nurtured my father. But it's different when you see your parents doing something. It's a completely different feeling. I tell her, like, "Babe, I want a girlfriend, not a mother. Do as much as you can for me, but you don't have to do everything. I'm a grown man. I can help myself."

NAN: When Jessy came into my life, she changed everything: my job, my

Nan and Jessy

work, and even my thinking. I don't know; right now I think I love her.

JESSY: You think? Or you know you love me?

NAN: I know I love you.

JESSY: Two different words, you *think* or you *know*. Two words. I want to be sure.

> *Nan turns toward me and says, "A few months ago, she asked me how much I love her. I said, 'Not a hundred percent.'*
>
> *"Jessy asked me, 'Why?'*
>
> *"I said, 'In real life, one has to live with a person before love moves to a higher level.'"*
>
> *Now Nan turns to Jessy. "YEAH! I know I love you, Jessy."*
>
> *Jessy pauses, quietly reflecting on his good fortune.*

JESSY: When most trans men go through transition, they don't want anything to do with femininity. They don't want anything to do with being a woman. They just want to be completely accepted in the straight world. When I first started my transition, I wanted it to be complete, from one side to the other. But now I'm embracing my in-between-ness. I'm embracing this whole mix that I have inside myself. And I'm happy. So forget the category. Just talk to me. Get to know me.

CHRISTINA
Every Girl Is Different

Christina's story begins on the #2 train, a subway line in New York City. It's late, about two a.m. Christina is a beautiful, tall, twenty-year-old college student whose long hair is sometimes dyed strawberry blond and sometimes dark brown. On this night, she and her boyfriend, Gabriel, are sitting quietly in their seats, minding their own business. Two girls across the aisle are giggling and chattering loud enough for others to hear.

Girl 1: I don't know what *that* is.

Girl 2: Yeah, what is *that*?

Christina: Are those girls talking about me?

Gabriel: Yeah, I think so.

Christina stares at them.

Girl 1: Hi? Can I help you with something?

Christina: Yeah, can you stop laughing at me?

Girl 1: This is a free country; I can laugh at whoever I want. And how do you know I'm laughing at-chu?

Christina: Because I'm not stupid. I heard you say, "I don't know what *that* is."

Girl 1: I know you're a man with that big-ass face.

Christina, anger rising, rapidly taps a foot on the floor.

Gabriel: You better learn to respect people.

Girl 1: I am being respectful. I said "hi," right?

Gabriel: No, you're not being respectful. You're over here giggling and laughing.

Girl 1: I can laugh at whatever I want. How 'bout you staying out of this and keep it between us girls.

Girl 1 makes quote marks with her fingers.

Christina: You better shut the fuck up before I fuck you up!

Girl 1: Who's going to fuck me up?

Christina: Me!

Christina throws her purse to the side, jumps up, grabs Girl 1 by the hair, pulls her off the seat, and punches her in the face. Girl 1 grabs hold of Christina's hair, but she is wearing a wig, so it comes off right in Girl 1's hand.

Girl 1: Fuuuuck!

Girl 1 throws the wig to the side and starts punching. Girl 2 pulls out a can of mace. Gabriel grabs her by the throat and throws her on the floor. By now the train is in chaos. The other riders try to break them up, everybody screaming.

When the train reaches the next station and screeches to a halt, Christina is thrown back on the seat. Girl 1 lands a right punch to her mouth. Christina's lip starts bleeding. Girl 1 then pounces on top of Christina, who is kicking, scratching, and trying hard not to cry. Eventually, the people on the train manage to break them up.

Girl 1: Yeah, yeah, you're bleeding!

She prances around the train, singing: "I fucked a man up. Go get your pussy the fuck off the train."

Christina

It was, like, I was trying not to cry, but it was really hurtful because . . .

Christina tries to hold back tears.

Thinking about that day again . . . one of many . . . people can be so nasty, so rude. I didn't do anything to her. She had to butt into my life for no reason.

I was picked on way too much to keep my mouth shut now. My mom is very worried that my temper could get me into trouble. I don't let people walk all over me no more, like they used to.

I've been called a man before. Even now, some girls say I look like a man. I don't know how they can pick it up, but they do. That makes me feel less a woman. I start questioning: Do I really pass in society? I don't want to get emotional.

The other day I was thinking, I really, really hate being a transgender. It's a constant struggle. It's so annoying. While everyone else my age is saving up for a car or a house, I'm saving up to look possible. I'm saving up for a vagina.

Me and my boyfriend, we've been having problems. And it sucks that I can't get over thinking that it's because I'm transgender. Like, how do you go all your life dating genetic women and then date a trans woman? Doesn't he miss a vagina? When a biological woman meets a man, she doesn't have to explain herself and hope that she will be accepted for who she is, unless she has an STD or something. When people see you they know that you're a woman, there's no question about it. But for me, that's something I have to explain and hope will be accepted.

When I go out I can't make any mistakes. My hair has to be exactly right. My makeup, my outfit, even my smell must be feminine. There are certain outfits that make me look more masculine than other ones. The other day, I bought a shirt that had ruffles on the shoulders. They made my shoulders look huge. So I can't wear that.

There were days when I would not go to school, knowing I damn well needed to get my butt to school 'cause I was on the verge of failing. My appearance stopped me. As I went outside I started to get panicky because I didn't feel right about the way I looked. I just turned back.

Christina's First Name

When I was born, I was named Matthew. Early on, when I was little, I felt that I wanted to be a girl, but I didn't have a full understanding about it. I knew I was a boy because my mom and my dad told me I was one.

When mom went to work, and my dad was in the living room watching TV, I would go into their bedroom with my brother Jonathan and play a game called Moolah. *Moolah* is slang for "money" in Spanish. The whole concept of the game was shopping. We would put on my mother's scarves and attach bobby pins here and there so that the scarves would come down really long. That was our hair.

I was about six, and Jonathan was seven or eight. One of us would play the cashier, and the other would be the shopper. We'd go around the room with pretend purses in our hands and say, "I want this, this, that." That was my idea about what girls do.

Christina has another brother, Elvin, who's eight years older.

Elvin would sometimes see us and tell my dad or mom, "They're acting like girls."

When my mom questioned us, I'd say, "I'm just a man with long hair." All my life I had an obsession with long hair. If we went to McDonald's and they were giving away little Barbies, I wanted the Barbie because of the hair.

My mom bought me and my brother lots of toys. When the movie *Pocahontas* came out, my mom bought me a John Smith doll, with his short hair, and my brother the Indian, with long, silky hair. I got really angry. In the middle of the night, I chopped the Indian's hair off. I did.

The teasing began in elementary school.

They called me a sissy and a faggot. I told my mom, and she wrote a letter to the teacher or the principal. It didn't embarrass me to get a bully in trouble, but I didn't want to have to keep going to my mom saying somebody's bothering me. That was embarrassing.

My brother Jonathan said, "You point out the kids to me, and I'm going to fuck them up." I was so afraid that things would escalate, and I didn't want my brother to get hurt. So I never said anything.

There was this girl in my elementary school in the fifth grade. All the boys were crazy about her. She was the *it* girl. She already had big boobs, a small waist, and a big butt. She was my ideal girl. I wanted to look like her. I wanted the attention from boys. She was tall. Her name was Christina. At that time I thought that if I was a girl, my name would be Christina. My mom hates that name.

Elementary school, when Christina was known as Matthew

Christina's mother loves her children very much. But she did not love the paths the younger two were taking. And she made no bones about it.

By the time Jonathan was eleven years old, he told me he was gay. When he turned twelve or thirteen, he told my mother and she completely flipped out. "That's disgusting!" she said, and started crying. Then she said to me, "I hope you're not gay too."

"No, I like girls," I told her. I was ten years old. What did I know?

My mother comes from a Catholic family who always went to church. She had no idea that Jonathan was gay. You can't tell unless you pay close attention to his eyebrows or something because they're really plucked. I was even shocked when he told me. I was very, very shocked.

Once my mom found out, everything started changing for my brother. He started dressing more feminine. He wore more colors. He brought gay people to the house. My mom wanted to be supportive, but she couldn't. She went to church and prayed for him. She cried over it. I have no idea if she spoke to the priest, but she did speak with her sisters. They all said, "He'll come out of it. It's just a phase." Bull crap!

I really was close to my extended family, but not anymore. They are just so narrow-minded. Every time I go over to my grandmother's house, they want to pray for me. I really don't need to be prayed for.

I was always feminine. Even in my early teens, I was feminine. I'd ask my mom, "How come my voice isn't getting deep?"

"Oh, you're just a late bloomer. Eventually, you will get a deep voice." But I never did.

Boys' High School

Christina begged her mother not to send her to an all-boys Catholic school. Her mother insisted.

At least send me to a coed Catholic school. She didn't want to do that. She was under the assumption that I was straight—straight but feminine.

My oldest brother, Elvin, had gone to an all-boys Catholic school, where he became disciplined and focused. So off I went to Mount Saint Michael Academy, a Catholic school for boys.

I was so nervous. Before I went there, I asked my gay brother, Jonathan, "How do I act like a man?" He would tell me I had to walk a certain way, like the hoodlums on the street, walking with a little lean, like, a little ghetto, gangsta boy. I practiced.

Jonathan said, "You have to change your clothes style too."

"Okay, what do I have to wear?"

"You have to wear baggy pants. You have to wear oversize T-shirts, a do-rag, and sneakers." Ugh! Everything I was not interested in! I liked wearing simple T-shirts with jeans. I'd look at girls' clothes and think, *Oh, my God, I wish I could wear that!*

Jonathan taught me how to sit with my legs open, which I could never do naturally. I hated it. It was the most uncomfortable feeling in the world for me. It looked gross.

Nothing came naturally to me. He told me I had to deepen my voice a little bit and talk like a man. That was kinda hard to keep up.

High-school freshman

When I walked into the all-boys school that first day, I felt I had done everything Jonathan taught me. I said, "Oh, hey, what's up? My name is Matthew. Oh, what's your name?" I wore baggy pants. It came off so phony; it just wasn't me. At all!

No one accepted me as a straight boy. Within a week, they started picking up that I was naturally feminine, a quiet kid, a shy kid. When I talked, I moved my hands around. When I drank something, I put my pinkie finger up. Those are not exactly masculine traits.

People started talking. "I think he's gay." One boy who was nasty called me a faggot. I would stand in the courtyard in the school, and someone would beam double-A batteries at me, just to hurt me. If someone beams double-A batteries at you, it's going to hurt. They would throw branches and twigs at me. They didn't do it to my face. They would just toss it and act like it wasn't them.

Once the kids started picking on me, calling me names, I needed somewhere to go and vent. I went to the school counselors. I had four counselors in four years. I trusted all of them because I assumed they were professionals. And they were. They helped me a lot.

37

Eventually I did find somebody to be my friend. Christopher. Christopher was a very feminine boy who liked Britney Spears, just like me. I had the feeling he was gay. When I asked him, though, he said he wasn't. He played it up that he was a straight boy, but I wasn't buying it. Eventually he came out to me and he became my best gay friend. He wasn't transgender. He was just gay. We still talk to this day.

Hoay is my best straight boy friend. I used to be very attracted to Hoay. When I was in my androgynous stage, I told him on several occasions, "I like you a lot."

"I don't go that way," he said.

I'd say, "But I'm a girl." That was something he couldn't grasp. I don't blame him. He met me as a boy, so I can't expect him to see me completely as a girl. He accepts me as a girl now, but I don't know if he completely sees me as one. He treats me like a girl. He's protective. I've heard from other people that Hoay really cares about me and worries about me a lot. But I don't think he would ever want to be with me.

I've gotten over that whole attraction to him. I see him as my brother. I'm glad to have him as one of the high-school friends I still talk to.

Gym—Last One Picked

The school gave us Mount Saint Michael T-shirts for gym class. We had Mount Saint Michael shorts, and of course had to wear sneakers. Ugh! I was okay about going to the locker room, but I felt uncomfortable changing in front of people. I had hairy legs, and I couldn't shave them because for one, I didn't want my mom asking questions, and two, I didn't want to make myself more of an outcast. It felt so nasty to have hairy legs.

At that time I tried to blend in. I had a little mustache, more like peach fuzz, that I eventually shaved off because I didn't like it. I was still trying to convince people I was straight. (But by my senior year, I was wearing spandex to gym class.)

I'd go to the corner to change because I didn't want to take off my pants. I'd keep the T-shirt under my button-down 'cause I never wanted to take off my shirt in front of the other guys. I didn't feel that I was exposing my breasts, 'cause I didn't have them yet. I just never liked to be seen with my shirt off. It made me feel uncomfortable. No one laughed at me. The only time they started laughing at me was in my senior year when I started dressing like a woman.

After everybody changed, we'd all go upstairs to the gymnasium and sit on our spots. The instructor, Mr. Valentino — I really hated him so much — there need to be more understanding gym teachers, there really do — he would make me do push-ups and sit-ups. We'd run around the track or play basketball. I told them I had asthma and I couldn't run. This is the truth. I do have asthma. But I also didn't want to run.

Then when we played basketball, I was always picked last. The teacher would place me on a team, and the boys would get upset, not because I was feminine but because I just couldn't play. I didn't know how to dribble the ball. I didn't shoot. I had never played these things. My dad would take me to a park and try to teach me, but I was never interested. I didn't want to ride bikes. I didn't want to play football. I didn't want to play Frisbee. None of that! I wanted to shop. I've been drawn to shopping all my life.

I wasn't really interested in learning, I just did what I had to do, and that was that. If there was a test, I'd study, but I wasn't interested in English or history. I was interested in art and fashion. I guess I was good at it. I did what I had to do and was on the honor roll and dean's list all four years.

I wasn't a reader. I read *Cosmo*. I read *Glamour*. For some reason, my mom didn't think much of it. She was in denial.

Drawing Beautiful Girls

I drew girls a lot. That's all I drew. To this day, I draw girls. I'm so into looking good and beautiful, and I'm always trying to figure out the next thing to make me more feminine.

One of the school counselors said, "I want to see your sketchbook. I want to see your art."

"Sure." I showed her pictures of girl after girl after girl — different kinds of girls. She said, "You know, when people draw, it's kind of like a way of escaping. People draw what they want to be."

The moment she said that — I had never spoken to her about transgender issues; I just said that I was gay and that people disliked me, they hated me—the moment she said that, I started thinking, *Well, yeah, I want to be a girl, but it will never happen.*

I told her that I wished I had been born a girl, but I knew it would never happen. If it did happen, I'd worry about passing. "I don't want people wondering what I am. I don't want to get hurt. So I'm definitely not going to do anything about it." And she was, like, "Okay."

But always in the back of my mind, I wished I was a girl.

Boys' Retreat

In my eleventh-grade year, I went with my class on a boys' retreat. On the retreat we all had to admit something, or say something we needed help with from God, because, after all, it was a Catholic retreat. I told everybody that I just want acceptance from everyone because I'm gay. By that time, I knew I wanted to be a woman, but I said that I was a gay boy because it was easier. The room was silent. I was so nervous. It was the first time I actually came out to people that I was different.

I think that's why some of the boys later had trouble understanding my transition. In my eleventh-grade year, I said I was gay, and in my senior year, I said that I was a girl.

I learned about transgender people when my brother Jonathan was dating a boy named Renee. No, I take that back. I learned about it when my brother started cross-dressing. He would dress up in women's clothes. He put on a wig and filled up bags with rice and put them in a bra. He went out in seven-inch stilettos and really short shorts. I found it really weird. We would play photo shoots in my house when my mom and dad were gone. This was when we were in our teens. I was about sixteen. He was seventeen.

He's not a cross-dresser now. I think he was trying to figure himself out too. He went from acting very straight, to very feminine, to cross-dressing, to straight-acting again. That was his process.

I asked him, "Could I look like a girl too?" My brother said, "No, you could never look like a girl."

"Let me try." I went into the bathroom and put on everything he put on. I looked in the mirror and thought I was the most beautiful girl in the world. I became Christina. I walked out of the bathroom to show my brother.

I just felt so, so indescribable. I was happy. Here I was, sixteen, still in high school, and feeling great.

He said, "You don't look like a girl. I really don't think you can pass as a girl."

"Well, I think I do."

There came a time when I had to take everything off. That really, really hurt. It was sad to see Christina go away.

My brother was dating a boy whose mother was transgender. He said, "My boyfriend's mom is transgender. She dresses like a girl and everything. She has the boobs and the hair and the body." When he showed me a picture of her, I was like, Wow, it is actually possible to change into a woman.

I can't remember exactly when I did it, but one day I typed *transsexual* into Google. *Transsexual* is another way of saying transgender. The site said, "When a man or a woman, or vice versa, feels that they were born in the wrong body, and they want to be the opposite sex." And there were a whole list of things, like, if you want to wear women's clothes, if you wish you were born a woman—I can't really remember everything exactly— but if you are these things, then you're transgender. This connected with me.

I thought, *Maybe it's possible that I can do this.* But I wasn't sure how to take the leap forward, especially because my mom still thought I was straight. I didn't want to hurt her feelings. I didn't want her to start going crazy or emotionally disown me. She didn't disown my brother, but it kind of, like, felt that he was disowned. It did.

My dad didn't care. He's a very accepting, very open person. When Jonathan came out to my mom, she said, "Don't you dare tell your father! He's going to flip out."

My brother was, like, "I told dad before I told you! And *he* took it way better than you ever did." My mom was really surprised. I mean, I'm telling you, nobody had a clue about Jonathan.

• • •

I saw another counselor, a man, at my school. He asked, "Matthew, how do you see your life?"

"I don't know. I just want to finish college and get a job and have a husband. I just want to be a housewife. I want to cook and I want to clean. I want to take care of the kids. I want to do all that."

"You know what you sound like? You sound like a traditional woman."

"What do you mean?"

"Everything that you're saying is from a woman's perspective. Staying home, cooking, taking care of kids. That's what women do, traditionally. That's what they were known to do."

"Okay, then, I guess I'm a traditional woman."

At that point, I had done my research. I told him, "I want to be a woman, but I'm very scared to do it. I'm afraid I'd be rejected by society, and that would make my life worse."

"Well, whatever you do, you should do it after high school."

"Okay."

Then I read that if you wait too long, the hormones are not going to be as effective. If you take hormones at sixteen, you're basically going through another puberty stage. When you take hormones at forty, it kind of doesn't have the same effect. When you're sixteen, you're still growing. If you replace your hormones, you won't grow as tall or your bones won't be as big. That's why I wish I had started at sixteen. I wouldn't be so tall. I didn't get hormones until I was eighteen, which is when Callen-Lorde allows you to do it.

At this point, only my school counselor and my brother knew that I was planning to transition. My brother knew a lot of transgender girls. He took me around to the Village (Greenwich Village), the Village Pier on Christopher Street, where there are lots transgender girls. They fascinated me. They looked so real. This has always been my worry: Am I going to look real? I don't want to *not* look real, because, I mean, what's the point?

That summer, right before her senior year at the all-boys high school, Christina decided to become female. She stopped worrying about what her mother would think. She was going to do what she needed to do, what she had to do.

What's My Purpose?

When I told my best friend, Hoay, that I wanted to become a girl, he said, "No, don't do that."

"Why not?"

"Because God made you a boy for a reason. And if he made you this way, it's for a purpose."

"Well, what's my purpose? I have no idea what my purpose is as a boy. I'm not going to have a kid. I'm not going to marry a woman."

"You told me that you are gay and now you're saying you're transgender. Why can't you just be a gay man?"

I told him that I *thought* that I was gay because I was attracted to men. But I'm attracted to straight men, not gay men. Before I educated myself about what being transgender really is, I thought that I must be a gay person.

The Google site said, "Sexual orientation has nothing to do with gender identity. There are gay transgenders and there are straight transgenders."

That was something really hard for the boys to grasp. It took at least two years for Hoay to get accustomed to calling me *she,* to actually believe I was a woman, to see me as a woman.

Gender Bending

Transitioning is a very long process. We go through stages. First we look like a man. Then we go through gender bending. And eventually we look like a woman. Gender bending is when you don't look like a male and you don't look like a female. You're changing from one gender to another.

My hair was short. With short hair, I looked like a boy. I had to grow it out. Because I was gender bending, I started to dress feminine. But I still looked like a boy. People would say to me, "What are you?" Total strangers.

I loved the attention back then. It's really weird. It's really weird because now if people think I'm a man, it sometimes turns me into a very violent person. I've gotten into countless fights with people.

Christina says this calmly while laughing at herself.

I know — that's masculine.

Becoming Christina

My hair grew long pretty fast. I dyed it red, cut it to my jaw, and then got bangs. I had to shave constantly—ugh, that's so annoying. I wore tighter clothes, but they were boy clothes. I didn't plan on telling my mom. I wanted her to figure it out for herself.

I tried to think of ways to make me look more feminine. I bought a lot of pink things. The thing that made my mom think I was gay was that my cell phone was attached to a key chain that had pink beads, hearts, and a little bunny. It was clearly for a girl.

My mom said, "We're going to your godparents' house. Can you do me a favor and take that thing off your phone?"

"Why? Why can't I have this on my phone?"

She said, "Because that's for girls."

"Who said this is for girls? Why can't a boy have it? There's nothing wrong with that."

She got fed up. "Okay, Matthew, I know you're gay. But that doesn't mean you have to show the whole world you're gay."

"Actually, Mom, I'm not gay."

"You like girls?"

"No."

"So you like boys?" She looked so confused.

"Yeah."

"So you're gay."

"No, I'm not."

"Well, what are you?"

"Have you ever seen those people on *Maury*? The *Maury* show? Have you ever seen those people? *'Is it a guy? Is it a girl?'* Well, that's me. I'm transgender."

"What is that?"

"I have a gender identity disorder, and I want to become a girl." (I had diagnosed myself.)

She was, like, "Okaaaaay, can you do me a favor and try not to show it as much?"

"Okay." I did her a favor and took the bunny off my cell phone.

• • •

Sometimes I feel that my mom misses her son. She doesn't tell me, but my brother told me he heard her crying about it one night. She misses her son. I told her, "I'm still the same person. I just look different." I don't understand why she feels the way she does because I'm not a parent.

Once my mom knew, it was time to start making my moves. I told my dad. He said, "I always knew it." I started crying because I had been so scared of his reaction. He said, "I love you. It doesn't matter to me. I knew since you were a little kid that you always wanted to be a girl. And I knew it was coming." He's great.

Senior year was fast approaching, and I had a lot of work to do.

The Best of Times, The Worst of Times

My senior year was my best and worst year in high school. The day before school started, I got my nails done. Pink. It was the first time I got my nails done, and I was so excited about it. To hide them from my mom, I walked around the house like this.

Christina curls her hands into a fist to hide her nails.

Eventually, my mom saw my nails and completely freaked out about it. "*Oh, my God,* why did you get your nails done?"

"Because I wanted to."

"You're going to get in trouble. You're going to get hurt. Somebody's going to hurt you, baby." She wanted me to take them off.

"No, Mom, I'll be fine." They were acrylic, and I was not going to take them off.

I was so excited about the first day of school. I was so excited that I was actually starting the transition. I blew out my hair. I put on my makeup: purple eye shadow, mascara, blush, lip liner, and lipstick. Put on my blue button-down shirt, my tie, and my khaki pants. Seniors are required to wear gray sweaters. Before school started, I took my sweater to the tailor and said I wanted to make it tight and feminine. He made it really tight for me. Everybody else's sweaters were baggy.

That first day I walked outside, people just stared at me. I loved the attention. I didn't think I looked like a girl yet, but there was something about people acknowledging me, wondering what I was, that made me happy.

I walked through the school gate and into the auditorium. People's jaws dropped. I walked down the aisle, saying, "Hi . . . hi there . . . oh, hey." I was so happy. I wasn't worried anymore. I was being me.

People were going, "What *is* he doing?"

The principal was telling us what classes to go to. I just sat there, so happy, with my purse — my big, black purse. I walked to class swinging it, and my friend was going, "What the fuck are you doing?"

"I'm a girl."

"Okay, you're crazy."

"Well, I just want to be a girl."

And he was, like, "But aren't you gay?"

"No, actually, I'm not gay. I'm transgender."

He couldn't grasp the fact. He thought a boy dressing in girls' clothes is gay. Period. Whatever.

As I walked down the hall, the freshmen were entering the school. When one freshman saw me, he was, like, "Hey, Mami, you looking so good. What are you doing here?"

I was, like, "Oh, my God, I guess I look like a girl!"

A big smile fills Christina's face.

So many of the freshmen were hitting on me. I guess they were being macho. Finally one of the older boys told the younger ones, "That's not a girl. She's a *he,* a senior." And they all started laughing at that boy, saying that he was gay because he hit on me. They were making fun of him.

Guilty Pleasures

I quickly became the school's joke. It was really the underclassmen that had a problem with me. They found my female MySpace account — I had a MySpace account as a woman and I had a MySpace account as a man.

My cross-dressing pictures were on the female account. There, I first introduced myself as Christina. I used that account to talk as a woman to different men. It was my way of escaping reality while I was in what I call my androgynous phase.

Someone in the school—to this day I don't know who did it—found that account and printed out all my crossing pictures. They posted them all over the hallways. It didn't bother me. I said, "Oh, look at me! I'm so pretty in those pictures." I looked great in those pictures. I liked the attention. It was guilty pleasure. It's really weird. I was so comfortable transitioning, I was happy to actually begin. Whenever boys gave me attention, good or bad, they were recognizing my femininity. That made me really happy. The only thing that bothered me was when somebody wrote *fag* on my picture. Somebody also wrote it on my locker.

People didn't know how to take what I was doing. They were shocked—including teachers and the principal. The principal called me to the office. He and the dean wanted to talk to me.

"Matthew, you need to cut your hair," the principal said.

"Why?"

"Because that's school policy. You have to keep it above the collar."

"Okay, I'll keep it above the collar."

"And you need to get rid of those bangs."

"But what's wrong with bangs? They're above my collar."

"No, you have to read the rules. It says no bangs."

"Okay, fine," I said, "I'll sweep it to the side. But I'm not getting rid of my bangs." The dean, the principal, and me have always had a problem.

Dress Down Day

Dress Down Day is when you don't have to wear a uniform. You can wear whatever you want. *Dress Down Day?* I came into school my usual self—makeup, hair done, nails on—and I wore a pink sweater, a girls' American Eagle sweater. I wore my mom's jeans; I actually fit into my mom's jeans, but they were really tight around the butt and hips. And I wore these flats from Payless that I had bought. At that point, I started progressively buying women's clothes and throwing out the boys' clothes.

I wasn't taking hormones yet. I was waiting. I had gone to Callen-Lorde and started counseling. Their rule is that you have to be eighteen and take counseling for four months before you get hormones.

I sat down in homeroom and took out my makeup bag. I was putting on my mascara, which always embarrassed my friends. "Matthew, don't do that shit here. What are you doing?"

"I don't care what people think. I'm going to do what I want." And on the loudspeaker comes, *"Please send Matthew V. to the principal's office. NOW!"*

And everybody was going, "Oooooh, you're going to get in trouble."

I thought, *Whatever.*

I walked into the office and said, "Hi, did you need me for something?" Again, the dean was there; the principal was there. The principal said, "Yeah, why are you dressed like this?"

"Because I want to dress like this. It's Dress Down Day. I can wear whatever I want."

"Well, you can't come to school dressed like a woman."

"Well, I am a woman." He got really angry. He slammed his hand on the table, "YOU'RE A BOY! YOU'RE NOT A WOMAN! YOU'RE A BOY!"

I started crying at that point. I said, "Actually, I am a girl. You just need to educate yourself. Get on Google and Google *transsexual,* 'cause I'm a girl."

He said, "You're creating this whole problem, this whole circus. Anything that happens to you is your fault, because you're coming to school dressed like a clown!"

I was crying—I'm still crying.

He said, "You need to go home and change into boys' clothes."

"Well, I don't have any boys' clothes. So if you buy me boys' clothes, then I'll wear them."

"Then I guess you need to go home and stay home and you cannot come to school on any other Dress Down Day."

"Fine! That's a day off for me."

The dean was a little calmer, a little nicer. The principal was a straight-up asshole. I hated him.

The dean said, "Look, Matthew, if you're a girl, why do you have to show it now?"

"Because I'm not waiting for nothing. I'm not waiting for high school to be over. I want this done now! I'm starting now!"

"But why the nails?"

"Why can't I have nails?"

"Well, you know you can't be wearing nails to school."

"But it's not in the handbook. If it's not in the handbook, that means I can wear nails."

"I'm sorry, but we didn't think that would be an issue."

"Well, now you know. Next year you need to put it in the handbook. Till then, I'm going to wear my nails."

"But why do you need to wear so much makeup?"

"Because it's not in the handbook, so I can do it."

The dean said, "Again, we didn't think we had to address these things because it's all boys here. We assumed that this would not be an issue."

"Well, you can't assume; you need to put it in the handbook."

"But my wife doesn't even wear that much makeup."

"Every girl is different."

I told him, "You know what? You guys, you need to understand: I'm transgender. I feel like a woman. I don't feel like a boy. This is what I want to do. There are other transgender people in this school who are afraid to come out."

Other students had come up to me privately and told me that they feel like a woman but that they couldn't show it because of school, because of their mom, because they were scared. I'd tell them that I was there once. "You just have to give it a shot. There's nothing they can really do to you." That's what life is about, taking chances. You're not going to get anywhere if you don't give it a try.

I think the other students were freaked out because I looked like a girl and I was pressing against gender boundaries. There were some instances when I'd be walking up the stairs and people thought I was a girl. "Oh, there's a girl here? Oh, wait, that's that weird kid."

In art class the teacher told us to hang up our paintings in the cafeteria while the underclassmen were having lunch. I was immediately worried. I told Hoay, who was in the class, "I'm really nervous. I feel like they might throw something at me." He told me to relax and just hang up my artwork. Lo and behold, when I walked into the cafeteria, everyone took immediate notice of me. I was kinda hard to miss with my red hair. Then slowly but surely I started to hear, "Boo, booo, boooo, booooo." It got louder and louder, and more intense.

Then they started shouting, "You don't belong here. Go somewhere else. Get out! Faggot."

The teachers tried to calm everyone down. I gave my art to Hoay, and I walked out, smiling. I tried hard to hold back my tears. I was smiling because I didn't want them to see me mad. That would mean I was losing and they were winning. It did hurt, though. So many people hated me for no reason.

Christina begins to cry. After a few moments, a composed Christina says, "When the going gets tough, what do tough girls do? We go shopping!"

After a few hours of shopping, we settle down for a lunch in a noisy Korean restaurant. Christina knows I'm curious about her high-school years.

I remember religion class—oh, I hated religion class—one kid raised his hand while we were talking about sexuality. He said, "I think it's okay for somebody to be gay. But why can't they just be gay and not turn into a woman? If you change your sex, that's a whole other level." Of course the kids knew I was in the classroom, and the boy next to me said, "You're going to take that? You're just going to let him say something like that?"

The teacher knew there was going to be a problem because by that point I was really standing up for myself. I wasn't going to take anybody's crap anymore.

So I raised my hand and said, "Well, for your information, being transgender is different from being gay. Being transgender is feeling like a woman. Gay men don't want to become women. They're men. They like being men, and they like other men. Transgender has nothing to do with sexuality at all. There are transgender girls that like girls. There are transgender girls who like boys. How do you explain that?" The kid had some snide remark, but I can't remember what it was. The professor immediately changed the subject.

I wasn't afraid to explain who I was. I like educating people. I don't like people staying narrow-minded and ignorant and stupid.

There was another time when I was sitting with my friend Christopher, the gay one, in class. Christopher had a very feminine voice, high pitched, and he could be very flamboyant at times. This boy in front of me, his name was Andrew, called Christopher a faggot for no reason.

I stick up for my friends, especially if they can't stick up for themselves. He was, like, taking it. I tapped Andrew's shoulder and said, "Why don't you just leave him the fuck alone?"

And he said, "Shut the fuck up! You're a faggot too."

"What did you say?"

"*You're a faggot! You're a faggot!* You're fucking gay."

"The reason you have a problem with this," I explained slowly, "is that you're gay and you're insecure about your own sexuality."

We started arguing back and forth while the teacher was trying to teach class. The teacher looked over and asked, "Hey, what's going on over there?"

And Andrew said, "Get this faggot away from me!"

The teacher said, "Matthew, can you get up from your seat and move to the back?"

I got really upset. When I got up, I pushed my table, and the desk just flew over. I guess Andrew felt threatened about that. He got up and punched me in my face. Then he threw me between the desks and was stomping on my head and back. Andrew was a football player and very strong.

The teacher didn't try to break us up. He ran into the hallway and called for help. I don't know who he was calling help for because we didn't have any security guards. At least the other boys didn't join in.

I had to go into the nurse's office because I was bleeding from my lip, always my lip. I had scratches on my face too. Even though I was angry about the fight, I was really angry that he had popped off my nail. I was mad. I didn't get a chance to hit him back.

I told my mom. We got him expelled and arrested. I eventually dropped the charges 'cause I just wanted him out of the school. I never saw him again.

I never cried in school until I got into that fight. After that I'd cry when some boy called me ugly or said I was not a woman. My friend Hoay would be there for me, patting me on the back, like, "Don't cry. It's okay." Getting teased every day was getting hard on me.

Deep into my senior year, I went home after school and I sat in the dark with music playing. I listened to an Alicia Keys song called "Caged Bird." The lyrics made me cry. My mom opened the door and asked, "Why are you crying?" I just burst into tears, telling her how hard it is to be transgender. "I feel like the world is against me. I want to become a woman."

My mom asked if I wanted to go to another school, but I thought, *What's the point? I'm in my senior year. If I switched, then these guys won,* and I didn't want them to win. They wanted me to leave school. They *really* wanted me to leave. They kept saying, "You don't belong here. You belong in a girls' school," which made me feel good.

People treated me like I was a disease. If there was a crowd of boys, I could literally go like this.

Christina stretches out her arms like Moses parting the water.

And the boys would jump back. "Don't touch it—you might get it!" they would say about me.

I enjoyed that. I enjoyed the attention. I'd be with my friends and say, "Wanna see a really cool thing I can do?"

"Yeah."

"Watch this!" So I'd move my hands toward the boys, and they would jump back.

There was one teacher, a math teacher, who would stare at me. I would sit in class putting my lip gloss on and think, *What is this guy looking at?* I always took stares as negative. Once the class was leaving, he pulled me to the side. "What is all this? Why are you putting lip gloss on and stuff?"

"Because I'm a woman."

He was smiling at me. "Yeah, I noticed that. What's going to be your name?"

"Christina."

"Okay, Christina, have a good day."

He was the only teacher who was nice to me.

Blue-Moon Sex Drives

It wasn't until I was done with the four-month therapy program that I could take hormones. In March, my senior year, I started taking hormones. They started changing me fast. When I first started taking them, I got very, very sick. I felt weak. I got headaches. I went to my psychology teacher, because in class we studied neurons and synapses and how our bodies react to certain medicines. I asked him, "If you change your hormones from one sex to the next, do you become sick?"

"You can become sick because your body's not used to it. Estrogen is foreign to your body. You have some estrogen but not much." My doctor told me to let my body get used to it. I might be sick for a month. And I was.

When I had testosterone in my body, I was a very horny boy. Before I went on hormones, I was able to get an erection and maintain one. Whenever I saw a boy I liked in the hallway or in gym class—the locker room is the best place to get my eyes on flesh—I'd get it. I think that's why a lot of gay people like to have sex. They're both men, they both have a lot of testosterone. It's kind of a manly thing.

The estrogen slowed down my sex drive. It's not that I had no sex drive; I have it once in a blue moon. My boyfriend feels like I'm not attracted to him. Of course I'm attracted to him. I just don't have the want or the need or the urge for sex all the time.

There are certain things that turn me on, but most of the time I don't want to have sex. I always wanted foreplay and romantic attention. My boyfriend was never the foreplay, romantic type. He just wanted to get right to it. What are you gonna do?

I'm glad I no longer have all that testosterone that fueled me to want sex. Normally guys can get it up with a cold wind. That doesn't happen to me anymore. I don't have the morning wood. I only have it when I'm aroused.

It's kind of weird: I know what it's like to be a man, and I know what it's like to be a woman. That whole testosterone-driven thing is something they can't really help. I'm happier without having that sex drive. The constant need for sex is annoying—it really is. I just realized that right now.

You know what I also realized right now? I know what it's like to be in the boys' bathroom and I know what it's like to be in the girls' bathroom. I think the boys are way more disgusting than the girls.

By April, my breasts started growing. I was surprised and excited. I was the only boy in class with tight shirts and budding breasts. Everyone wanted to touch them. Of course I let them. It just feels like flesh; it feels like nothing.

Then the time came when I first put on a bra. Now, that scared me! It was so uncomfortable. I had been going the whole year flat-chested. I was comfortable being a gender bender, not yet comfortable being a girl. Once I put on a bra, I knew this was it. That was when people needed to see me as a girl.

Before I put on the bra, I told my friends, "If you want to call me Christina, great. If you want to call me Matthew, that's fine too. But once I make full transition, don't you dare call me Matthew."

. . .

In the beginning of my transition, I would literally panic if I didn't get my hormone shot. Now I forget to take it. I say, "Oh, I'll do it tomorrow. I'll do it next week." I'm trying to get back on a schedule. I took it two weeks ago. I take it every two weeks and that's annoying. I hate it with all my heart. The thing is biological girls don't have to do that. They don't have to put a shot in their thigh just to maintain their figure. But because I'm transgender, I have this constant worry.

I can tell when I don't take my shot because I start to feel physical changes. I start to lose my shape, my hourglass. My skin feels rougher. I grow facial hair quicker.

During Christina's gender-bending stage, people were attacking her right and left. Christina's mother was having a very hard time dealing with one gay son and another who was becoming a daughter. But Christina was unhappy and in danger.

Her mom says, "At that time Christina still had the features of a man. She was dressing like a girl, but she didn't look like a girl. It was very hard. Imagine me waiting for her to come home. I was always afraid something happened to her: somebody attacked her, or somebody said something to her. I said, 'Baby, you can't wear so much makeup. You can't do that. You're in a boys' school.' She's a fighter. She fought. That's how I taught her."

In spite of her feelings and reservations, Christina's mother pulled out her credit card and bought her daughter breast implants. "Now she looks more like a woman," Christina's mom says proudly. And the bond between mother and daughter grew stronger.

I used to go to the gym a lot but I stopped 'cause I was losing my hips. That looked masculine. And there it goes again with my whole fear of being all man. I started eating more to gain back my hips. I didn't want to end up like my friend, a transgender girl who's so worried about looking male, she's afraid to go outside.

Senior Prom

An announcement over the loudspeaker: *"Let me remind you: You cannot bring a same-sex person to the prom. You cannot wear a dress to the prom."*

And everybody started laughing when they announced that. "Oops, sorry, Matthew, you can't wear a dress." It was so annoying.

"Okay, I may not be wearing a dress, but I definitely am going to look like a girl." I bought a woman's tuxedo that was curved at the waist, and it made me look hourglass. I wore a pink button-down shirt, open. I bought one-inch, peep-toe heels. I got my hair done and extensions put in to make my hair look long. I had my nails done and my makeup and my eyebrows and everything. I thought I looked great. I was so happy. My friend Josephine, who I've known since first or second grade, came with me.

I think the prom was a good experience. I had a lot of fun, actually. By that point a lot of the seniors accepted me and we were friends. Even if they weren't my friends, they treated me with respect. The majority that hated me was the underclassmen. But the seniors had been with me for four years. They had grown accustomed to me at that point. Did they agree with what I was doing? No. But they were, like, "Well, that's Matthew."

After the prom, we took a boat ride. The captain said, "Girls in this line. Boys on that line." I thought, *Let me try this out,* and I went on the girls' line. All my guy friends were saying, *"That's not fair!* Why are you on the girls' line?" But they were just poking fun at me because the girls got to go onboard first.

When the guys got on, I was already dancing. I rubbed it in their faces. "I got on the boat first because I'm a girl. I got on the girls' line. Ha, ha, ha."

Nobody questioned it. That felt great. For the first time in my life, I went on the girls' line and was not told I had to be on the boys' line.

Never Forget Me

Graduation was such an exciting thing for me. It was annoying that my mom wouldn't let me wear my weave. I think she was still a little embarrassed about me, but she didn't want to admit it. It sounds wrong to say, "I'm embarrassed about my own child." But I knew that she was. She didn't want me to get my nails done, but I did. She didn't want me wearing makeup, but I did.

When I walked down the aisle, all the parents were taking pictures of me. Of me! I'm sure their sons had told them about me. Some wanted me to stand alongside their sons when they took pictures. Others wanted to take their own picture with me. One father told me, "You're the first girl to graduate an all-boys school."

"I am," I told him. And he just took a picture of me. I felt great when he said that. I was making history for Mount. *They will never forget me.*

Actually, they took me off their mailing list.

High-school graduation

Sometime after I graduated, I asked one of the boys, "How was Mount Saint Michael after I left?"

He said, "You wouldn't believe how many people started coming out of the closet." I felt great about that. Even when I first came out, many others started to come out. So many. And I had a lot more friends because of it.

Once Christina turned eighteen, after graduation and just before college, she legally changed her name.

My mom was lying in bed one day and I said, "Mom, I'm going tomorrow to legally change my name to Christina." And she was, like, "Okay." She didn't think I was serious.

The next day when I came back with my papers and everything, she said, "Your name is really Christina? Baby, why didn't you tell me so we could talk about a name?"

"Yeah, Mom, I told you." My mom hates my name. I mean, I also changed my middle name to Jayleen, the name she would have given me if I was born her daughter. I gave her that!

My mom said that I was changing what she named me. But I couldn't walk around with the name Matthew.

59

College Girl

At FIT (Fashion Institute of Technology) everyone welcomed me with open arms, even when I told them I was transgender. I'm completely girl here. But there are no straight boys at this school. They are all gay. I wanted to experience being a girl and falling in love.

Women at a very early age are taught not to be hos, not to let anybody touch them, not to let anyone disrespect them. Well, I don't know anything about that 'cause I wasn't raised a girl. As far as exposing my body, I wasn't really taught not to do that.

I'm learning to be female. A lot of times trans women dress very sexy to get attention from men. If a man hits on them, says how beautiful they are, in their minds they look passable.

I do it too. I dress sexy. I used to be borderline ho. But that's not what most women do, 'cause women are comfortable with themselves; they know that they're women. But a trans woman, me, is trying to convince herself by showing skin and being sexy.

I wanted to experience being a girl and falling in love. None of my transgender friends have boyfriends. There's one girl who made a video saying that no man is ever going to take a trans girl serious. That's what I feel. He's going to want to have sex with a trans girl, to see what it's like, but at the end of the day, he's going to put the ring on the genetic female.

Whenever my transgender friends get a boyfriend, I say, "I give it one month, or two." When a man finds out you're trans, his respect for you goes down. If a man meets me as a woman, he's very nice, gentle, opens the door for me, and doesn't talk about sex. As soon as he finds out I'm trans, he starts talking about sex. It's frustrating because he's not treating me like a woman anymore. It makes me less a woman.

I'm learning how to deal with men. I talk about men a lot. I do. Right? Don't I? I keep going back to men, boys . . . terrible.

When I started dating straight men, it was very scary to admit that I was transgender. They could get very violent and freak out. Or they could say they didn't care. But I always doubt that people are genuine when they say they don't care. What's their motive? Sex? I feel that no man takes a trans woman seriously at all.

Christina at Fashion Institute of Technology

Talking to guys, telling them that I'm trans, gets old so fast. They ask stupid questions, like, "How do we have sex?"

I get mad when they ask me that, but I can't blame them for their ignorance. If they've never had an experience with a trans woman, then how can they know? But that shouldn't be the first question that comes out of their mouths.

They ask me so many questions that are very personal, like, Do I still have it? Do I still have my part?

If I did get to the point where I felt comfortable talking about it, I would say, "You know, it's just like doing it with a regular female, only I don't have the lady part." They can use common sense to figure out what that means.

Sometimes they ask me, "Am I gay for liking you?"

I have to get accustomed to men paying the bill. I'm used to "I pay my part; you pay your part." But on dates they'll say, "No, I'll pay the bill."

At first I felt bad about it because I felt that I didn't deserve to have a man pay for my meal. We were both getting to know each other, so why did he have to pay for it? I also had to get accustomed to a man holding a door open for me. I had to get accustomed to a man walking on the outside of the street. That was very, very weird.

Christina's Sometime-Serious Boyfriend

My mom never spoke to me about sex. She didn't talk to my brothers, either. I feel that if I had been a girl, she would have spoken to me about it. I learned from my own experiences that I was getting nowhere having sex with different guys. When I did, no one took me seriously. I learned that in order for a man to take you serious, and love you for you, you can't have sex with him right away. When I met Gabriel, he didn't believe me when I told him I was trans. He thought I was just saying that.

He tried to have sex with me right away, but I didn't let him, not until he said, "I want you to be my girlfriend." I wanted to be sure he was really serious. We didn't have sex for two months. I wanted to see if he truly liked me for me and not because of the way I look.

I can't truly let myself go with him. I've been in bed with my boyfriend, but I never let him see *it*. Ever. I wear my panties the whole time when we're intimate. And that really sucks because I can't be fully intimate with him. I'm always worried he's going to see it; he's going to feel it.

Gabriel went against his own family for me. At first they didn't know that I was trans and they loved me; they thought I was a great person. One of his cousins went to Mount Saint Michael. He went on my Facebook page and saw that I used to go to Mount. It was easy to put two and two together.

He told my business to Gabriel's whole family. Once they found out I was transgender, they said, "Don't let her in my house."

Gabriel stood up to them. "I love her. I'm not leaving her."

I've been with my boyfriend for three and a half years, and that's because I put up with his bullshit a lot. Right now we're on a break. I can't help but think that he wants to be with another girl. He's done this to me so many times. Once, I had gone out with another guy and he cheated on me too. Girls get cheated on all the time.

If I had been born a girl, I would have had lots more boyfriends. If I had been born a female, I could leave Gabriel. I have mixed feelings about this. There are so many things I love about him. He's accepted me. When people in the street call me a man, he's never embarrassed. How am I going to find that again?

Friends, Pronouns, and Vaginas

All my trans friends with vaginas look beautiful. They got everything they wanted. It would be so great if I could get an operation, if I could get my vagina. It will be great to get that over with and live my life. I feel like I'm not truly living my life yet. I'm living it fifty percent. If I had my surgery, I would live it to the fullest.

I still hang out with boys from Mount Saint Michael. They're straight. I went to a house party recently where there were a lot of Mount boys. I came in and announced, "Learn your pronouns because I don't want to have to slap somebody tonight."

They said "hi," and gave me kisses on the cheek. I was surprised. I was really happy. That showed me they accept me as a woman.

They didn't give me no pound. There was one boy who put his hand out like that, and I said, "I don't do that."

He was, like, "Oh."

"I'll take a handshake, but I'm not going to do that."

I won't do the hand bump, either. Michelle Obama may do it, but not me. They're doing that to me because they probably still see me as a man, like, "What's up, bro!"

There was a boy at the house party; he was like a rocker boy who called everyone *dude.* With me you have to walk on eggshells with that word. I take it very defensively—especially when there's alcohol involved at the party.

When I was drinking he called me *dude* and I took it the wrong way. I told him, "Don't call me dude, 'cause I'm *not* a boy." And he was like, "I'm sorry, I'm sorry. I'm just trying to help you out." I was really drunk.

I was with my friend Hoay because we still hang out; we talk all the time. So the rocker went up to Hoay and said, "You need to watch out for him." Him being *me.*

I got up out of my seat and said, "Don't call me *dude!*" and I put my hands around his neck and started backing him up against the wall. Everybody was pulling me off him.

"Relax, relax," he said. "I'm just trying to help you."

People were saying, "That's not very ladylike."

"Well, people gotta learn," I said. I mean people are not going to learn anything if there is no consequence to it. If you're nice to people, they're not going to take you serious.

The next day, he told me that he didn't mean to call me *him* or *dude* or anything like that. It's just that he wasn't used to me. I'm not around him much.

I am around Hoay a lot, so when Hoay calls me *he,* I scold him.

I saw the rocker again at the next house party. He said, "Hey, Christina, how are you?" He was being nice to me and gave me a kiss on the cheek.

Sometimes I see Matthew in the mirror. Sometimes, on my lazy days, when I'm just lounging around the house with no makeup on or anything, I see him.

Once I put on my boyfriend's clothes to see what it was like. I pulled

my hair up and put on his do-rag. All I could see was my face. I must admit I was very happy with what I saw in the mirror. Although I had on boys' clothes, I still looked super feminine. I had my breasts, and my hips were poking through the sides of his jeans. My boyfriend told me that I looked like a lesbian; I didn't look like a boy at all. He can't imagine me as a boy. I was so happy about that.

"Hold on! Hold on! I have something to say," Christina's mom says. "After all, I'm the one who had the problem with this."

Christina's Mother

Christina and Jonathan are my children, and I love my children regardless. I would never throw them out into the street like some parents do. Some families throw their kids out and they get into prostitution and they wind up dead. I would never, ever do that. I told them, "Baby, not for nothing, I'm glad that you guys are proud to be gay or transsexual. But you can't let people know." I had a lot of learning to do.

Christina was always very sensitive. I couldn't yell at her the way I yell at my other sons, Elvin and Jonathan. She was crying all the time! All the time!

"Will you stop crying?"

Even the lady upstairs heard it. "What are you doing to him?"

"Nothing! He just cries at every little thing."

Jonathan was wearing women's clothes long before Christina came out transgender. He was cross-dressing. That was very hard for me. I said, "Okay, Jonathan, you are gay, but you don't need to dress like a woman."

My next-door neighbor told me that she saw Jonathan dressed as a woman outside. When I confronted him, he said, "No, Mom, not me. I never dressed outside."

I thought that was a phase he was going through, because after a while he stopped that altogether. Right now he's very masculine. He works out; he's very husky.

I was telling Jonathan, I said, "Jonathan, do you think Matthew—that was Christina's name—is gay also?"

And he would tell me, "Mom, time will tell."

As a child, Christina didn't tell me much about how she felt. I found out that she was transsexual the second year of high school, when she was sixteen. That's when I noticed certain things about her and I actually thought that she was gay. Her movements—she was acting different—the way she was walking, the things that she liked, and she started wearing makeup.

She said that she wore makeup because she was breaking out a lot. She said that she was covering up her acne. She was going through puberty. But the truth was, she was transitioning. I had no idea.

Matthew Becomes Christina

Matthew was at Mount Saint Michael's, and that was a problem. He was letting his hair grow long. I thought that he was gay, like my other son.

One time I found him crying. I said, "It's okay, it's okay. I know that you're gay."

"No, Mom, I'm not gay. I'm transsexual. I feel like a woman inside."

That was shocking to me. I didn't know what that was. "What do you mean, you feel like a girl inside?"

"Mom, I feel like a woman inside."

"Okay, okay."

I spoke to my family about it. They were even more in shock than I was. Nobody exactly knew what a transsexual was. I have a huge family, seven sisters and three brothers. One of my sisters said, "Wanda, I thought Matthew was gay. I saw some indications. I saw the way Matthew moved." At the time he was obese; he was very obese. She's still a big girl. So I just thought she had her little moves because obese people tend to move in a certain way.

Most of my family accepts Matthew as Christina. But my older brother in particular does not accept her because he's religious. He thinks there's a bad spirit in both my children, that there's no such thing as being born that way. I don't want to disrespect my brother, but I tell my mother, "Ma, did you see that program on the Spanish channel about transgender? That they are born this way?" Christina doesn't want to see her uncle.

67

I worry about her when she's not home. She'll call me on the phone, crying, "Mom, I got into this situation!"

We live in a six-building complex. Once she called me: "Mom, some guy punched me in the face!"

"Are you okay?" I got all upset.

"'Yes, Mom, I'm fine.'" She called the police. I believe she pressed charges. My son started looking for the guy. A few weeks later, I was coming out of my building and saw a whole bunch of men. I said to myself, *Maybe that's one of the guys who attacked my daughter.* I just walked between them and said, "I want to know who attacked my daughter. Be a man and come out."

One man was looking down, and I had a feeling it was him. I told him off. I said, "What is it your business that my daughter is who she is? My daughter goes to college. My daughter works. My daughter goes to an internship. My daughter isn't bothering anybody. Have you ever seen her bother anybody here? Why is this your business?"

He finally looked up and said, "I was the one."

"How dare you! How dare you attack my child! What has she done to you?" And I started criticizing him. I said, "Look at you! Are you jealous of my child? My child as a man *and* as a woman is handsome and beautiful."

I think he was a foreigner. I said, "You're not from here, right? In America people are used to this. There are gays, there are lesbians, there's transgender. There are all kinds."

The other guys said, "Don't worry, ma'am. From now on, we're going to have respect for her. We're going to watch out for her."

And yet there's always one issue or another that can pop up at any moment and spoil the day.

When Christina got her breast implants, I was relieved because she looked more like a woman. But when I'm in the train with her, I still hear little kids say, "Mom, is that a man or a woman?" I don't want to hear that. I sometimes have to remind her not to show her Adam's apple, and that's so sad. I don't want to have to remind her to keep her chin down.

• • •

Christina's very intelligent; she can understand difficult things. But something simple? She can't do it. I tried to teach Christina how to wash her clothes. I tried to teach her how to cook. "I don't want to, Mom." I think she's a little lazy about things like that. But as for makeup, she teaches me. She'll do my hair. Being that she's into fashion, it comes natural.

I go to her and say, "Christina, how does this look? Should I do this? Should I do that?" And she tells me.

It's different having a daughter. The other day I bought dye to color my hair. When I went to look for the dye, it was not there. I said to myself, *I know I'm not going crazy. I know I bought the dye.* Well, guess who took my dye?

She dyes her hair all the time. I got angry with her. I said, "Baby—I call her *baby*—you can't be doing this to me. I was getting ready to dye my hair, and you took my dye." She takes my mousse. Everything is in her room.

But then she takes off her weave and leaves it on my bed. That part I don't like about having a daughter. She's very messy. She wasn't messy as a boy. You should see her room. No, it's too embarrassing.

Jonathan Comes Out

I took Jonathan's situation a lot harder than Christina's because it was new to me. Jonathan's situation helped me with Christina. Jonathan was only thirteen years old when he came out of the closet. I feel bad to this day that the first words that came out of my mouth were "That's disgusting!"

I insulted him so bad. That was a horrible thing to do. I have apologized to him. I hope he knows how sorry I am.

When Jonathan started making his little gay moves, we had a problem. We went to counseling and we used to argue right there. My issues were he was doing the hand movements and talking like gay people. I said, "You know what? The day before you told me you were gay, you sounded like a normal teenage boy. All of a sudden, one day later, you're sounding like gay people. You're moving like gay people. I don't want you to do that. I don't want it because you'll be in danger. You'll get attacked."

He argued with me. "No, this is who I am and this is how I move." I fought so much with him about that.

Christina and her mom

Jonathan was at Mount Saint Michael's too, but he couldn't take it. He purposefully failed his classes to get thrown out. So I moved him to a school for gay, lesbian, and transgender students. In the beginning it was rough for me. I had to go to parent-teacher conferences. I did not want to be there. I was still not used to the idea of a gay son. There were guys dressing up like girls, and I would give them dirty looks. They would act flamboyant, and it would kill me. I felt it was not necessary. *Oh my god, they're not girls, why are they acting this way?*

Jonathan would bring flamboyant boys home, and that would kill me too. Now I accept anyone who comes to my home. I love them because I know they don't get enough love from their parents.

Jonathan was overweight, and he started going to the gym. Now he's a body builder, and very good-looking. *Very* good-looking.

Don't be like I was with Jonathan. Don't say horrible things to your child. That will haunt me till the day I die. Hug your children. Hug them.

Christina's mom cries softly. "I'm sorry," she says, wiping away tears.

I learned through Christina. I didn't read a book or call anyone for information. I listened to my daughter. And I learned by letting her be.

Mariah requested that no
photographs be included
in her chapter.

MARIAH
The Real Deal

Place: The Moonstruck Diner, New York City
Time: Noon

On a sunny spring day in June, Mariah, nineteen, arrives at the diner exactly on time. Her close-cropped, curly black hair and olive-almond skin surrounds the bone structure of a model. Eyes, big and round, remind me of a Madonna in a Renaissance painting. I wish I had brought along my professional camera rather than the click-click sleeping somewhere in my bag.

This day Mariah is wearing a pale-pink man-tailored shirt and khaki pants. "I'm dressing gender neutral," she tells me while we walk to a booth in the back of the restaurant, "because I'm not comfortable with my body. I don't want my picture in the book. I'm telling the truth about my life because I think you should know about me and my community. But I'm not ready for people to see me."

Oh, no! I say to myself, hoping against hope that she will change her mind. We find an empty booth and order lunch.

Mariah's voice is like honey sliding down a spoon. "My social worker—we usually make jokes—she says, 'You talk like woman, you act like woman, you look like woman, but you eat like man.'"

Mariah goes on to say that she is not in a good place. "I'm not a success story right now. I'm just starting to transition my name to Mariah. I want to go to college and live in the city. Anywhere but Long Island! I have too much bad history in Long Island. I want to go somewhere where nobody knows me."

Although she is taking her hormone shots every two weeks, Mariah does not consider her transition effective. "I know I will never have a period, I will never have a uterus, I will never have fallopian tubes, and I will never have ovaries. I will never have those things, so technically I will never be a woman. What's the point of having a vagina when I can't have those things? I wanted to experience what real women like you experience. Inserting a tampon. Of course, I can insert a tampon when I get a vagina, but what's the use of it?"

"Believe me, it's not so great," I reply.

"Everybody says that," Mariah says softly, smiling. "But you know, when it comes to us, it doesn't matter if it feels great. It makes us feel real. It makes us feel like the real deal."

Mariah

My story is a little bit different. You may hear transgender people say that when they were little, they felt different; they were born a boy but felt like a girl. When I was little, I believed I actually *was* a girl. I really did. I didn't know the difference between a boy and a girl. I noticed that kids dressed different and played different games. I didn't think it was a gender thing, because I was a girl.

I'm biracial. My mother is black and Cherokee Indian, and my father is an immigrated Italian. My mother passed away when I was ten, but I'll tell you more about that later. I never knew my father. I believe he's still alive; he's not in my life.

I lived with my mother and my grandmother, but I can't say they raised me. Placement raised me. I've been in the system all my life. When I turned eighteen, I signed myself out. I'll be twenty next month.

Let's start when I was a kid.

This Boy Wears Dresses

When I was four or five, I wore girl clothes. My grandmother took a lot of heat for it. It wasn't her fault. It was my way of expressing who I was, because that's who I thought I was.

Around the time I turned five, some guy on the street said, "Yo! You're not supposed to be wearing those clothes."

"Why not?" I always got defensive about this 'cause everyone was always telling me this.

"Because you have a dick."

"What's a dick?" I didn't know what that was.

"Boys have dicks and girls have pussies."

"Well, what's a pussy?"

"A vagina."

"Bagina?" I didn't even know how to say the word.

"No. *Vuh*gina."

"Oh, okay."

Then he said, "So you're not a girl. You have dick."

"Well, what is a dick?"

"That thing that you have between your legs."

And I'm, like, "I thought everybody has that."

"No, not everybody has that."

I thought, *This man is crazy.*

A lot of people didn't approve of me. My neighbors cursed out my family. "You're raising a fucking boy! He's supposed to be wearing fucking boy clothes, not fucking girl clothes. You should go to jail for this shit." That's what they were saying.

None of my friends teased me when I wore girls' clothes. They were cool. There were things I liked doing as a boy, and there were things I like doing as a girl. As a boy, I liked to play outside, ride my bike, and get a little dirty. I liked cars. I was hyperactive. I liked to throw things. I never really liked action figures; I never liked to pretend with G.I. Joe, and this and that.

On the girls' side, I liked Barbie dolls. I liked brushing their hair, braiding it. I liked to have pretend tea parties, being pretty, trying on makeup.

• • •

I grew up in a bad neighborhood. There was a lot of violence—not guns—knives. There was a lot of alcohol and drugs, but only when my mother and her friends were home. You learn what you see, so I used to fight a lot. I wasn't a punk.

"Who's a punk in kindergarten?" I ask, and we laugh at the notion.

My grandma's short and fat and passive. She's not the kind of person who will argue. She never spoke her mind. Like an old-fashioned woman, she kept her thoughts to herself. Don't argue. Whatever is said is done. I don't like that about her—it would make me mad.

She was a teacher for twenty years, and then she worked for the county for ten years. She has a master's degree. It's very weird. I don't understand how she could be educated and end up in the 'hood, the ghetto, a poor neighborhood.

She was married once, long before I was born, but her husband died in a car crash. I think she was traumatized. Years later she adopted my mother.

About the time when most children started talking, Mariah did not talk at all. Social workers thought that she might be underdeveloped. Instead of going to public school, Mariah was sent to a special ed. school, Variety Child Learning Center, in Syosset, Long Island.

I didn't like the school. I was trying to be myself, dressing the way I felt, and I was getting punished for it. The first day of school, my teacher looked at me, surprised, and I thought, "What is going on?"

She said, "You're a boy. You're not supposed to go to school like this. Don't put on these clothes again! You're not supposed to do this."

She had a look, like, "What's up with the parents?" I was thinking, *Why is she looking at me like that?*

I didn't say nothing, but I continued to go to school the way I wanted. I used to like wearing these jellies. They looked like princess shoes, and I loved them.

I remember one day the teacher took me out of the classroom and pinched me hard. I didn't like that. She said, "What's going on with you?

You're a guy! Are your parents abusing you? Are you being raped? Are you being molested?"

As a five-year-old, I didn't know what those words meant. She wouldn't stop. "This is not right. You're not supposed to be doing this. I can't believe you're doing this." And she looked very sad, like I was her child.

She took me to another room and tried to force me to tell her what was going on. And she would pinch me more, trying to find answers. That was her way of interrogating me. I thought, *Stop! Stop! Please stop! This is what I do. This is who I am.*

Mariah says that her teachers could not control her, so they brought in psychologists and the social services department.

The teacher reported me to DSS (the Department of Social Services). We were under investigation. My grandma was charged with abuse and neglect for me wearing girl clothes, and I was placed in CPS (Child Protective Services).

Thinking back about it now, I can't believe how something so simple as my clothes led to people thinking that I was being abused, that I was being molested. No one was forcing me to do nothing. My mother and grandmother also bought me boys' clothes. And I would wear them. I mean, I liked being a boy, but I liked being a girl too.

You know, I think a lot of this was my fault. I wasn't a kid who listened. I didn't listen to nobody. And my grandma wasn't the kind of person who would put her foot down and say, "No!" If I yelled and cried because I wanted something, she'd give it to me. That was my little secret—yelling. I would go into a temper tantrum, and eventually I got what I wanted.

My family found a way to edge me off girls' clothes. They said, "Okay, if you go to school with boys' clothes on, you can wear a little dress under it."

"Okay."

So basically I had boys' clothes on and a V-cut dress under it. Or I'd completely wear guy clothes and then little heels. I remember wearing my jellies with shorts.

Bizarre Behavior

When I turned six, my behavior became really bizarre. I began threatening people to get what I wanted. I would tell my grandmother, "If you don't buy me this or that, I'll run away!" I yelled and screamed and even threatened her with a knife. Can you believe that? She sent me to a doctor, who diagnosed me with ADD.

When Mariah was diagnosed with ADD, attention deficit disorder, she was put on Ritalin, the first of many prescribed drugs.

My mother had nothing to do with me. She was not in the picture. She was living in the house, but she'd go in and out. She didn't pay attention to me. I thought she didn't care about me.

I think the reason why I wore girls clothes, my mother's clothes, was to have a bond with her. My mother was an alcoholic, she was on drugs, she was a prostitute, and she also had lupus. She taught me some things, but basically she left me with my grandmother. I wanted to have a bond with her, and I also wanted to be a girl. I loved the idea of being pretty, of being a princess. I loved the idea of Barbie and beauty. I just liked dresses! But a lot of people didn't approve of it.

After Mariah threatened her grandmother with the knife, the social workers had her committed to a hospital. Her grandmother was grateful.

My grandmother thought I needed help. Help! Help! I was not being cared for. A person who isn't cared for? Come on. Of course they're going to act out.

There had to be an excuse to get help from the government. First they put me in a hospital. I was in my hospital clothes all day, a gown with an opening in the back. I liked that.

There was this girl there. I thought about that guy in my neighborhood telling me that girls have vaginas. I looked at her and thought, *This must be a girl.* So I went up to her and told her I liked her and she said she liked me. We started kissing. I picked up her skirt and looked in her underwear. "Where's your dick?"

"What's a dick?"

"You don't have what I have."

"Well, what do I have?"

And I put my hand down there and felt this little hole-kind-of-thing. I got really scared and ran away. At the time, I thought girls must have had their dicks cut off. That's what makes them a girl.

I was so scared, I didn't know what to do. I sure didn't hang around her no more. Then one day, when I was with my mother or my grandmother or maybe it was the social worker—I don't remember—I said, "I want to have my dick cut off, because I want to be a girl."

But then I got over that phase and thought, *Nah, I don't really want that. I want boy clothes.* So I stayed with the gender I was born into, but I still had urges for girl clothes.

Still, I grew out my hair and had girl hairstyles. I would see a dress or a purse at the mall and force my grandmother to buy it. "You can put them on, but don't go outside in them," my grandmother would say. But I looked so pretty. I wanted to show people what I was doing.

First Grade, Things Got Weird

The first or second grade is when things started getting pretty weird. I was seven at the time, living at home, and going to a new school in a black community. I'm not a racist, but when it comes to queer people, black people are very ghetto, as I would say. In my low-income community, people had no education and no jobs. They were grown-ups acting like children. The adults, not the children, made fun of me when I wore my wigs.

Mariah did not wear dresses outside, but she loved to go out wearing long hair, barrettes, and beads.

And I wore girl boots with heels too. Sometimes I wore stilettos that I took from my mother. I acted like I was beautiful. The kids wouldn't say nothing 'cause I was a fighter and they was scared of me.

But the adults were not scared.

"You're a little boy! What's going on wit' you? You're not supposed to be wearing girl clothes. Take that shit off, boy." And they'd laugh. Or when they'd see me, they were, like, "Come here, girl. See this!" and they'd start laughing.

I guess I had more courage than I have now. When I'm home now, I only wear boy clothes.

I was sexually mature. What I mean by sexually mature is that I knew about sex. From six up, I used to kiss other guys in my neighborhood, make out with them, and perform oral sex on them. I liked it. I used to love oral. And I touched their you-know-whats. We were really young, but that's what we did.

I was making out with girls too. I used to love making out with girls 'cause everybody thought I was cool. Everybody was encouraging me. "Look, Frank's not gay—he's making out with a girl!" They wanted to know how the hell I learned to kiss like that. I didn't know how I learned. It was pretty weird.

Guys used to hit on me—perverts—pedophiles. I'd see guys giving me a look, and it kinda creeped me out. They would touch themselves, saying, "Come here, sweetie." Something told me not to go. I ran away. I ran to where there was a lot of people.

By then, I hated being a kid. I had a grown-up's mind and thought I was an adult. I acted like I was an adult. I got into adult conversations. I wasn't hanging around children no more; I was hanging around adults, people on the streets, neighbors, and my mom's friends. I used to sing and dance for them. I danced like a girl and like a boy. I just loved performing. But it was very, very strange. Why would a child hang around with adults so much? Why would adults hang around me? DSS was concerned about that too.

DSS was so concerned that Mariah was taken away from her grand-mother and put in a foster home for a month or so. Then she was moved to another foster home. Then another. Finally she was placed in a residential treatment center.

Placement

When I was about eight, I was put in placement. I went there 'cause there was a lot of allegations. The social workers reported that my behavior was getting really bizarre. They didn't tell me this at the time. They only said it was because my mother or my grandma couldn't take care of me. They said that my mother was neglectful. I didn't think so. But they just took me away. It was horrible, really traumatizing.

This placement place was called ANDRUS Children's Center, in Yonkers, New York. It used to be an orphanage, and then some rich man spent millions of dollars to turn it into a placement center. I forgot the whole story. It was an old English-style mansion that was built in the eighteen hundreds. It was beautiful. There were over twenty rooms. I had never seen anything so lavish.

There were fourteen or fifteen kids living in separate cottages, or units. A staff watched over us, but it wasn't like prison. It was like a boarding school, but it was not a boarding school.

This was one of the best places I had ever been to. The things I did there I probably never would have done had I stayed with my grandmother, to tell you the truth. She didn't have the money. She didn't have resources. She didn't have a car.

In placement, I couldn't wear girls' clothes and I actually accepted being a boy. I played sports and felt normal. But I always had these urges. I wanted long hair. I loved pretty dresses. I loved skirts.

I remember saying to myself, *I have to grow my hair to look like a girl so boys will like me.* Now, when I think back, I think, *Did I really say that back then? Did my body, my soul, know what I was supposed to be?*

At the time, though, Mariah accepted herself as a boy and fell in what she calls "kitty love" with another boy, Michael.

We were so close, like brothers. I don't know if he's gay—I haven't seen him in years. We'd play kitty games, like, every time we took showers, we'd take off our clothes and put towels around us. Michael would rip off my towel. "Stop ripping off my towel!" He was really sneaky about this. I would get really mad.

Then he'd do it to some of the other kids, and I actually had a jealousy feeling. I keep thinking, *What is this feeling?* I didn't know the word *jealousy*, only the feeling.

We would go on trips every day. We went ice-skating. I started biking. I saw animals in the zoo. We had a really good time.

Two staff members always went with us. One was Kathy, the recreation person, and the other was Franklin. He was Puerto Rican, and a lot of people told us we looked like each other 'cause I looked Spanish when I was a kid. And our names were almost the same, *Frank* and *Franklin.*

Because we all liked Kathy, anyone who Kathy liked, we liked. They were really good to us. No abuse. No abuse at all.

There was sex—what I would call curiosity sex. We were experimenting. Isn't that what a kid does at that age?

Michael and I became roommates, and we got really close. We told each other things about our parents. His mother was a crackhead. I told him certain things about my parents. Because I was a private person, people thought I was very mysterious. But back then I didn't know much about my family.

We'd share our clothes and share our CDs. At night, he used to get in bed with me and we'd kiss or hug each other.

On trips, I'd sleep on his lap in the van. I used to like that type of stuff.

Michael was a type-one diabetic. He had to test his blood, and he couldn't eat certain things. He used to give himself his own needle. We kids thought that was cool. Most kids are scared of needles. It was really cool to see him give himself a needle 'cause none of us could do it. Michael was a popular kid. In a way, I was popular too, but I was very quiet, a shy person. The staff loved me.

My mother died in 2001, just before the World Trade Center. It was around my birthday, July 6. I thought, *This is one bad birthday present.*

This is where my belief in God comes in the picture. When my mom passed away and I was told the news, I was really sad. I thought of one person on the staff who I wanted to take me to the funeral. Her name was Marie, and she treated me like I was her son. I loved her. I asked for Marie, but she had already gone home. Then, for some reason, she came back. I thought that I must have a guardian angel. It was so weird: she wasn't here, and all of a sudden, she appeared. I didn't know how to process it at that time, so I thought it must be God sending me a guardian angel.

After the funeral, I was scared to sleep in my own room. By that time, Michael had been discharged and I had my own room. I even had my own bathroom and walk-in closet. I didn't want to sleep where it was dark. I thought maybe I'd see my mother's presence again, and it scared me. I slept in the hallway.

I had always been afraid of my mother. Once she almost killed me. I don't know what I did to make her so mad. I always had an attitude, a bad mouth, a fresh mouth. I was really rude and snotty. I don't know what I did, but she started throwing seven or eight beer bottles at me. One hit my back, one almost hit my head, and I was running for my life. She could have killed me. No one called the police, because the neighbors stopped her from trying to kill me. I still have a little scar on my back. What mother throws glass beer bottles at a child? Who does that?

I realized how weird my life was: wearing girl clothes, *feeling* I was a girl, *thinking* I was a girl. ANDRUS brought normalcy into my life. I didn't mind being a boy. I liked being tough and playing sports. And I wasn't scared of bugs. I felt like a cool kid. But still, I loved to watch someone's hair being done. I loved looking at dresses. I accepted that I wasn't supposed to do that, but I still fantasized about it.

I asked my teacher, "Why do girls call each other 'girlfriends,' but I can't call my friends 'boyfriends'?" I got in a little trouble for that.

The teacher sent me out of the room just because I asked that question. I didn't think I was saying anything wrong. I thought I was being logical. I guess they knew my case and they didn't want me to regress. They didn't want me to go back to doing girls' stuff. Stop him in his tracks! That's the only explanation. Why would they send me to a time-out room for this?

Back with Grandma

When I turned eleven, I left ANDRUS and went home to live with my grandma. To tell the truth, I was a monster at the time. I was really frustrated.

I missed being at ANDRUS, where I had friends, where it felt like I had family. At home, I didn't have no brothers. I didn't have no sisters. It was just me and my grandmother.

At my new school, people started picking on me. I never dealt with that before. It was the first time I felt lonely. That's a really hard feeling. I felt that everybody hated me. It made me depressed. It made me sad. It made me feel creepy. So I started acting out, cursing my grandmother again.

School made Mariah feel like a loser, so she acted like a loser.

I just started going off. Have you ever heard of kids who used to get picked on, whatever, and they became psychopaths? That wasn't me. I never became a psychopath. But I did go berserk. I made threats. I wanted to hurt their feelings. I was mad.

I threatened my teacher. To tell the truth, I actually pushed her to the floor—and she was pregnant. I know that was bad of me. I regret it. But she crossed the line. She was in my face all the time. She said that I threatened to blow up the school. This was after 9/11, so when a kid said that back then, it was a big deal. They called the police on me and made it seem I was a terrorist. I did say I wanted to set the school on fire and blow it up. But I was mad. I would never actually do it. I ended up back in the system.

First they sent me to a hospital, where I was diagnosed as a "bipolar, clinical psychopath with narcissistic tendencies." Can you believe that? That's crazy!

There were allegations that I was abusive, not good in school. The report said that I literally set the school on fire. I never did that! If I had set the school on fire, I would have been in jail. Come on! That's really a heinous crime, no matter how old you are. I didn't do that. I was just really mad.

At Nassau University Medical Center, a psychiatric center, Mariah was put on all kinds of medications.

It was horrible. It was like being at a cuckoo house. I was a zombie. The meds made me think slow, move slow. I had been one of the bright kids in my class. I'm not a genius, but I have good insights, and if I study, I'm really good. The medicine delayed my concentration. I couldn't do math. I couldn't write. I couldn't run. The medicine made me flip out.

I was not crazy. I knew it, but they didn't know it. And I was still acting up, still cursing people, and they go by your behavior.

State Hospitals — Drama Queen

When Mariah turned twelve, she was placed in a state hospital called Sagamore. She started gaining weight, lots and lots of weight.

I went from weighing ninety pounds to 120 . . . to 150 . . . to 175.

She was moved to yet another placement center, currently called MercyFirst, in Syosset, Long Island. At the time it was Saint Mary's Children's Center. Mariah hated that place. And then another weird thing happened.

I was starting to look like a girl. I had a girl's face and a high-pitched voice. My chest wasn't like a man's chest. I was growing women's boobs with large areolae. People would ask me if I was a girl, and I used to get mad.

Everybody else went from being a boy to being a man. It seemed like I was turning from being a boy to being a woman. Personally, I think it was all the medicines I was on. I was on a whole lot of meds.

How the hell does a boy start looking like a girl? Why?

Everybody else was getting deeper voices. Everybody else was getting facial hair. Everybody else was getting bigger penises.

Now I'm glad my penis is small. I've never even used it. But at the time, I wanted it to be big because I wanted to be with a girl. I told myself, *If I had a big dick, I'd be with a girl.*

I was still very popular. The staff loved me, and the kids loved me. But I was very emotional. I was a drama queen, crying all the time. I became a crybaby, clinging like a little boy to its mother — or a little girl.

I didn't like that about me. I tried my hardest to be a guy again. I played football and ran track. I tried to lose weight. No matter how hard I tried to be a guy, I looked like a girl. I was really pissed off.

Somebody said that if you drink liquor, you get a lower voice. I was drinking. It's hard to drink liquor when you're thirteen.

"Smoke cigarettes. It will make you have a deep voice," a friend told me. I was smoking cigarettes back to back to back to back. It didn't even work. It kinda lowered my voice a little. But I can't scream. I used to be able to scream, but I can't scream no more, so I guess it had a little effect.

The many medications made Mariah lethargic and slow-witted. Another patient there took advantage of her weakened state.

This guy got me to perform oral sex on him. I thought I was doing the right thing by performing on him. But I wasn't. He was just abusing me. He had total mind control over me. He didn't have to get physical with me; he just knew where to hit me where it hurts emotionally.

We finally got caught in the act, and I was very happy because I wanted it to stop. I think the directors were worried that they could get sued because they kept telling me it was consensual. It wasn't consensual at all. But I just wanted it to end. I wanted them to stop talking about it, so I agreed.

Afterward, that guy told everybody on campus about us, and they all thought I was this big old homo. Other kids tried to have sex with me. Other kids wanted to abuse me. I was so confused. I was mad at myself, slow because of the medication, and I didn't know what to do.

Becoming Mariah

When Mariah turned fourteen, she was still a resident at MercyFirst. She was attending summer school and had begun a summer job. Because she had no choice in an institution, she presented as male, but everybody thought of her as female. Although she had lost a lot of weight, she was quite chubby.

I still had my boobs.

Her body was curvy. The other students liked her, and she was feeling very good about herself.

I was happy.

A lot of boys were hitting on her, as if they somehow understood that she was indeed a girl.

I was the most popular girl on campus. I started home visits. I went home every weekend, Friday to Sunday. It seemed like everything was going good for me. I always wanted to go home, but I knew in reality home wasn't good for me. The only reason I wanted to go home was that was all I knew—that was my home.

In May, a new resident arrived. His name was Victor, Victor from Brooklyn.

There was an event going on and I was looking at him, going, *Wow, he's cute.* I really liked him. I would go up to him and talk to him and find a reason to be next to him. Our cottages were next to each other, and I remember looking at him through the window. I would look at him and smile, and he would smile back at me. I would skip school and go to the gym just to be around him, just to talk to him. I wanted to be his girlfriend. It didn't seem odd or quirky; it was natural. I was confident. I don't know where that came from because I didn't have a lot of confidence at the time.

Although they never had a physical relationship, Victor knew that Mariah was interested.

Well, one time he approached me. He said, "I'm told that you're really good at head." I was freaked out. I was excited. I was like, "Oh, my God!"

He said, "Well, why don't you do that to me?"

I said, "I would, but I have to go to work right now. When I come back, I will do it."

I remember walking with my work group and thinking, "Oh, my God, he wants to . . . you know . . . with me." I had butterflies in my stomach.

When I came back, I waited and waited for him. When I found him, I asked him if he wanted to do it, but he said, "I was joking."

And yet Mariah felt that they shared a strong connection. By the end of the summer, Victor was released from MercyFirst.

It could have happened if he had stayed there longer, and if I had made a move. But I was really nervous at the time. I wasn't how I am now. I was very shy. He was an older guy. He was seventeen or eighteen, and I was fourteen. I always felt that he was out of my league 'cause he was this really cute guy and I was this ugly, fat thing. Any girl could have had him.

After Victor left, a Mariah Carey album was playing. There was this song, "We Belong Together." Music never did it for me before, but when "We Belong Together" came on, I thought, *Oh, my God! Mariah Carey gets it.* That song talked to me. I love Mariah Carey. I'm a big fan.

Mariah Carey is so beautiful, and I remember thinking, *I want to look like that.* I went into my room and it suddenly clicked to me, *Frank, you're bisexual.*

I'm bisexual? It was like the wind blew in and hit me that I'm bisexual. I had a really good friend on staff at that time. Her name was Ruth. I went to see her.

"Miss Ruth, I think I'm bisexual, but don't tell anybody—I'm still new to it." See, I wasn't the type to be in the closet. I always told people who I was.

Once I was released from MercyFirst and moved home, I started acting more like a girl. I started losing weight. I started dancing. I wanted a straight guy. I fantasized that I was out with a sexy guy.

When I turned fifteen, I stopped taking my medication and started having panic attacks. I got into another fight with my grandma. I became very aggressive and severely depressed. Basically I was out of control— again.

I also got into a fight with some kid and broke a beer bottle on his head. He needed stitches. I got charged. I went to a juvenile detention center, then back to MercyFirst.

There was a staff woman there I fell in love with. Her name was Karen, and I used to look up to her. She had a very big butt. I used to target her. I'd curse at her. It wasn't because I hated her—I really liked her—I wanted her to be a part of my life.

I fantasized that I was a beautiful woman. I fantasized that I was Mariah Carey.

At first I changed my name to Monica because that was my mom's name. I guess I wanted her to be part of me. I fantasized that I was this very big star, a pop singer. I was Lady Gaga, and everybody loved my music.

I was open about being gay, but I wasn't open about being trans. To tell the truth, I didn't know the word. I knew that I wanted to be a girl. I knew that I wanted to be popular. I knew that I wanted to be cute. But I wasn't any of those things. I was actually pretty much a loser. I thought I was the only one in the world that was going through this. I didn't know about hormones yet. I didn't know what SRS was—sex reassignment surgery. I didn't know what the procedure was.

I started reading and hearing about other people like me. I was actually jealous. I thought I was the only one feeling like this. *Hey, how the hell you feeling like that?* I was mad about that.

It was funny and stupid at the same time, but I really wanted to feel special. *How can you be feeling the same things I'm feeling?* And it made me really mad, like, I'm not special after all.

I was sent to a new placement center, in Pennsylvania, where I worked with a good therapist. I told her I wanted to be a girl. She was an excellent social worker, one of the best I had had so far. She told me to write everything I felt in a journal. I wrote down all my fantasies. I don't think she wanted me to transition into girl; she wanted me to look inside myself, more than the outside of myself.

As I learned more, it made me feel sad, like I had a disorder. Transsexual. Even the name sounded weird to me. It was like I'm not born who I am; I have to transition to be who I am.

A lot of transgender girls feel that they look like a boy and they try to fix it. The thing is, real beauty comes from the inside. You could be the most passable trans woman ever. Real beauty from the inside! And that's what the therapist was basically telling me.

Guy to Guy

But then, at sixteen, guess what happened? I started going through male puberty. My stomach started changing. My head structure started changing. My legs started changing. My face. My eyes. I started getting facial hair.

I thought, *What is going on? I've always looked like a woman.*

The other kids were confused too. They looked at my face and asked, "What is this?"

"Oh, my God, I'm growing facial hair."

They were laughing at me. They weren't laughing at me to make fun of me. They knew I liked to be feminine.

I put Nair on my face. Stupid! It tells you on the bottle not to do it. But I put Nair on my face and it burnt me. Two weeks later, I noticed hair coming in, again, especially around my mustache.

I put Nair on again to remove it, but it started coming in stronger. I never had a full beard, but hairs were coming out all over and I was becoming more masculine.

What's going on with me? When I wanted to be a man, I looked like a woman. Now, when I want to be a woman, I'm turning into a man. Why?

God really doesn't like me.

I acted feminine 'cause I wanted to be a girl. I couldn't picture myself as a guy. When I was with a guy, it wasn't me being a guy with another guy. It was me being a girl with a guy. It was too confusing to tell everybody that, so the easiest thing to say was, "I'm gay."

I think it must be difficult for trans men who like guys. Most gay guys don't like vaginas. Have you ever seen an enlarged clitoris? It looks a little like a little penis. Most of the time gay guys aren't interested in that.

The guys I'm interested in are down-lows, DLs. That's somebody that says they are not gay but participates in gay activities, or are confused. Down-lows are basically gay guys still in the closet. They're people who live double lives or deny they are gay. Those are the guys I went out with.

Transition

A lot of people say I'm a dyke. I guess that's because I have feminine features but I wear guy clothes. I'm not ready to wear girl clothes yet. I live in a neighborhood that's not too accepting. And a lot of people know me too well for me to transition fully.

A lot of older transgender people say it's inside beauty that counts. And, you know, I usually agree with that. But we're young. We look at the magazines and we want to look like that. I want to look like Mariah Carey. She's black and white, just like me. I look up to her.

Transition starts when you feel that you're a woman physically, mentally, and emotionally. You fantasize about it. You research it. You start wearing women's clothes. Then you start looking into hormones. That's really transitioning.

I'm taking transition step by step. I told some people: my aunt, my cousins. I told my good neighbor. My grandma knows. She prefers me being a guy. But she can't change how I feel.

I've been on hormones for seven months. I think the hormones make me hungrier. Otherwise, I haven't noticed a big change. Well, maybe my skin is softer; my muscles are very soft, very flabby. I always had big breasts, so that's no change. I don't get erections as much as I used to. I never did much, anyway, because I never really liked my penis. I have a lot of stretch marks—my whole butt is one big old fat stretch mark. I have stretch marks on my hips, my thighs. It's terrible. I have to go to the gym. Actually, that's the estrogen at work.

With hormones, my facial hair doesn't grow back as fast as it used to. I had laser on my face—only four sessions and it worked pretty good.

Ever since I transitioned and accepted that I'm a girl, I've been attracted to girls. But they say that's not weird 'cause gender has nothing to do with sexuality.

I want people to know what I went through. I want people going through the same thing to know they are not alone. Transition? Everyone goes through one kind of transition or another. We go through transitions every day. Except mine is maybe a little more extreme. I'm not at the end of my transition. I'm barely at the beginning.

TRANSLATE TRANSCEND TRANSACT TRANCE TRANSCRIBE T
GURE TRANSPOSE **TRANSPORT** TRANSACT TRANSVESTITE T
RANSPIRE TRANSPLANT TRANSVERSE TRANSGENDER TRANS
SITIONAL TRANSGRESSOR TRANQUIL TRANSFORMATION T
RIPT TRANSMIT TRANSSEXUAL TRANSFER TRANSIT TRANSF
M TRANSFIX TRANSGRESS TRANSPARENCIES TRANSIENT TR
TRANSMISSION TRANSITORY TRANSLUCENT TRANSITION TRAN
LATE TRANSCEND TRANSACT TRANCE TRANSCRIBE TRANS
TRANSPOSE TRANSPORT TRANSACT **TRANSVESTITE** TRANS
PIRE TRANSPLANT TRANSVERSE TRANSGENDER TRANSMUTE
NAL TRANSGRESSOR TRANQUIL TRANSFORMATION TRA
TRANSMIT **TRANSSEXUAL** TRANSFER TRANSIT TRANSFIGU
TRANSFIX TRANSGRESS TRANSPARENCIES TRANSIENT TRA
ANSMISSION TRANSITORY **TRANSLUCENT** TRANSITION TRANSI
TRANSCEND TRANSACT TRANCE TRANSCRIBE TRANSCRIP
NSPOSE TRANSPORT TRANSACT TRANSVESTITE TRANSFORM
TRANSPLANT TRANSVERSE TRANSGENDER **TRANSMUTE** TR
TRANSGRESSOR TRANQUIL TRANSFORMATION TRANSLA
ANSMIT TRANSSEXUAL TRANSFER TRANSIT TRANSFIGURE T
NSFIX TRANSGRESS TRANSPARENCIES TRANSIENT TRANSPI
MISSION TRANSITORY TRANSLUCENT TRANSITION **TRANSITION**
ANSCEND TRANSACT **TRANCE** TRANSCRIBE TRANSCRIPT

SCRIPT TRANSMIT TRANSSEXUAL TRANSFER TRANSIT TR
NSFORM TRANSFIX TRANSGRESS TRANSPARENCIES TRANSIE
TE TRANSMISSION *TRANSITORY* TRANSLUCENT **TRANSITION** T
ANSLATE TRANSCEND TRANSACT TRANCE TRANSCRIBE TRA
RE TRANSPOSE TRANSPORT TRANSACT TRANSVESTITE TRANS
NSPIRE TRANSPLANT TRANSVERSE TRANSGENDER TRANSMU
ONAL TRANSGRESSOR **TRANQUIL** TRANSFORMATION TR
PT TRANSMIT TRANSSEXUAL TRANSFER **TRANSIT** TRANSFIG
M *TRANSFIX* TRANSGRESS TRANSPARENCIES TRANSIENT TR
RANSMISSION TRANSITORY TRANSLUCENT TRANSITION TRANS
ATE TRANSCEND TRANSACT TRANCE TRANSCRIBE TRANSC
TRANSPOSE TRANSPORT TRANSACT TRANSVESTITE TRANSF
PIRE TRANSPLANT TRANSVERSE **TRANSGENDER** TRANSMUTE
NAL TRANSGRESSOR TRANQUIL TRANSFORMATION TRANS
TRANSMIT TRANSSEXUAL TRANSFER TRANSIT TRANSFIGURE
RANSFIX **TRANSGRESS** TRANSPARENCIES **TRANSIENT** TRANS
SMISSION TRANSITORY TRANSLUCENT TRANSITION TRANSITIO
TRANSCEND TRANSACT TRANCE TRANSCRIBE TRANSCRIPT
ISPOSE TRANSPORT TRANSACT TRANSVESTITE **TRANSFORM**
TRANSPLANT **TRANSVERSE** TRANSGENDER TRANSMUTE TRA
TRANSGRESSOR TRANQUIL **TRANSFORMATION** TRANSLATE
SMIT TRANSSEXUAL TRANSFER TRANSIT TRANSFIGURE TRAN

CAMERON
Variables

Prom Night

It's gay prom night in Westchester County, New York, and sixteen-year-old Cameron, who prefers that I use the gender-neutral pronouns they, them, *and* their, *describes what they plan to wear — a man-tailored shirt and pants, with black leather and metal stilettos. "I'm not gender neutral, because stilettos are a pretty gender kind of shoe," they tell me. "And a button-down is a pretty gender kind of piece of clothing. It's more like — I don't know — am I allowed to curse? — I'm dressing gender fuck."*

"What's that?"

"Gender fuck is blending stuff, having something girl and something boy and something neither. The cords are pretty gender-neutral 'cause they are skinny and gray. The shoes are sexy. They're about four or five inches high and have a little platform, not a huge platform."

As we sip iced tea at a local diner, Cameron explains the difference between gender identity and sexual orientation. "Gender is one variable in a person's identity, and sexual orientation is another variable. The two are not connected. Being trans is not the next step to being gay. They are similar in that they are both breaking gender rules.

Gay people are breaking rules about who they are supposed to sleep with, and trans people are breaking rules about what gender they are supposed to be. I like to think that's obvious, but I guess it's not.

"You can be gay, bi, pan, homo flexible (mostly gay), hetero flexible (mostly straight), or just queer. If you are a homo flexible woman, you mostly like women with the occasional guy, the occasional gender-bender queer person. It's like, gay with exceptions."

These clear, sharp descriptions intensify my curiosity about the person sitting across the table. Who is Cameron?

"Mine is not the typical trans narrative that you see on TV. One of my best friends is trans and gay. I'm trans and pan. Pansexual. Basically I like people regardless of gender. I mean, of the people I'm attracted to, some of them are girls, some of them are boys, and some of them are not boys or girls. Actually, a lot of them are not boys or girls."

"Tell me."

My name is Cameron. My birth name is totally irrelevant. Honestly.

I started questioning my gender around my fourteenth birthday. And I probably started questioning the gender system around that time too. My first thought was that I was gender queer. Gender queer is not part of the gender binary, meaning somebody that's strictly a boy or strictly a girl.

Recently I began to feel comfortable saying that the gender system does not work because it really does not work for me. That's when I started defining myself as outside a gender system that society dictates.

Some people don't understand this. To them I just say, "I'm a boy; call me *he*." But I like to be recognized as not a boy and not a girl. I'm gender queer, gender fluid, and gender other.

As you can see, I think about this a lot. It's a pretty big part of my life. It's what sets me apart from the rest of the world. Since gender is everywhere in society, I've tried to understand it more profoundly. Why do girls wear pink? Why do boys wear blue? How does this whole gender system work?

When I started questioning my own gender, I realized that the notion of gender as commonly accepted wasn't a hundred percent true. And then, when I met other trans people and started reading trans literature, I realized that it *really* isn't true. Everybody can be everything. The best way to describe it is with pictures.

Someone Awesome

I'm from a town in Westchester County, New York, called Ossining. That's not one of the rich, white Westchester towns you hear about. It's really diverse, which is awesome. When I was in middle school, we moved to a village that's part Ossining and part its own thing. I'm still in Ossining school district, which is good because I hate the village part. It's really Waspy. I don't like being in the rich, white part of Westchester. It makes me uncomfortable.

My parents both majored in theater in college. My mom was studying to be an actress, and my dad was going to do lighting and build sets, a tech person. When my parents were in their mid-to-late twenties, they were living in Queens. There was a manhole fire right in front of their apartment. My dad brought the firefighters coffee. He started talking with them because he's a very social person.

The firefighters said that the entrance exam for the fire department was coming up and that you had to be under twenty-nine to take it. So he took the exam, became a firefighter, and now he's a battalion chief in New York City.

My mom is a social worker. She works with hospice. She helps dying people and their families. My mom has gotten to a place of understanding about trans people and parents of trans people so that she can help other parents accept their kids. Because she is a social worker, she already has the experience talking to families about things. But I like to think that part of her understanding is because of me—I've been able to explain things to her in a way she can understand. My mom is very cool.

So my parents don't have nine-to-five jobs. I think it's kind of interesting that both of them work for nonprofits. I think that not working for profit has affected their parenting and their life perspective. And it's helped me understand why you don't need to work for profit to be someone awesome. It's part of the *money isn't everything* thing.

Gender is more fluid and more complex than society assumes.

The easiest way to explain it is to draw a line to represent gender, with arrows at either end. Put an *M* on one end and an *F* on the other.

A person can be anywhere on the line. Or it's like a spectrum and you can be anywhere on the spectrum.

But for me, even describing it as a spectrum is too limiting because gender is explained as somewhere between girl and boy. That identifies gender the way society indicates, and that's not what it's about. There are other genders out there that don't fit onto the spectrum range.

Gender does not have endpoints; it's three-dimensional. Males float around somewhere, females float around somewhere else, and some people just don't float at
all — they swim.

What I mean is, unlike the floaters, swimmers control where they're going. The swimmers *do* their gender instead of *be* their gender. Or at least they direct their presentations.

And I guess that's what I do.

But I was kind of annoyed when my mom said, "I see someone else today." And you know who she was talking about? Me, before I came out. It was annoying because she was not looking at a different person; she was looking at a different gender.

Some days I'm masculine, and that's pretty weird. Some days I'm feminine, and that's pretty weird too.

A week ago, I wore a girl-cut T-shirt. It was a girly day.

I felt great about it.

I want to go to college so that I can go to med school so that I can help people so that I can do good stuff. Wanting to do good would not be something that would come easily to me if my parents worked in the corporate world.

They do wear suits. Well, my dad has to wear a uniform. He has this line of shirts in his closet and they are all exactly the same. There are about a dozen of them, uniform shirts. And he has to wear a specific shade of blue tie. Are you serious? I don't get that whole uniform thing. In some situations, sure, like, if you're in a marching band. Whatever. He's cool about it.

Then there's my brother. I have one brother, a year younger than me. More about him later.

A History of Weird

Whenever that nerd/regular split started happening, I was definitely, definitely on the nerd side. I wore knit pants, like yoga pants, cargos, and cords. I don't remember much about that. It wasn't important to me.

I was a girly kid. Really. I liked Barbies. I was a very, very oblivious girl. I was naive and very much into my own little bubble of fantasy books and that kind of stuff.

In preschool, I tried to teach the other kids how to draw because I thought I could draw better than they could. That continued into kindergarten and first grade.

In fourth grade, we had to read out loud from an English textbook, and I never followed along because they were reading slow and I was reading fast in my head. I was pissed off when the teacher called on me.

I didn't wear jeans until the fourth grade, and when I did wear jeans, I tried to tuck my T-shirt into my jeans. Nerdy.

My cousins would look at the way I dressed and say, "You're weird."

"Yeah, okay." They've been saying that since forever, so I have a history of being weird.

Fifth grade, I was the only kid in my class who actually liked our teacher 'cause he was big on writing and I was big on writing. Everyone else was annoyed about that.

A Bunch of Phases

When I was thirteen, I told my parents I was a lesbian. We were leaving for church and were sort of late. We go to a Unitarian Universalist church, so it's not like some big praying thing. I said, "Mom, Dad, there's something I have to tell you."

"What? We have to leave."

"I'm a lesbian."

"Okay, now get into the car."

That's a pretty chill thing because they were both in theater and know people who are gay. My brother's piano teacher is gay. And my dad's sister, who lives in Oregon, is gay, so big, stinking deal. They said that they had to come to terms with it, but it wasn't a huge thing.

In the seventh and eighth grades, I went through a bunch of phases trying to figure out where I fit in. What sort of niche could I find in this horrible middle-school world?

I hung out with a group of girls, semi-preppy, popular kids. They were not my people. In the seventh grade, the bubble popped. Bubbles don't pop all at once when we're talking about metaphorical bubbles. I don't think I saw things differently until the end of seventh grade.

One day at lunch, I didn't sit at the table with the girls. It wasn't something I thought about and thought about and thought about. It started out as a whim. I sat at another table, Noah's table, instead. He became a good friend. I'm president of GSA, he's vice president, and we're going to the gay prom as friends.

I don't remember how the girls reacted when I changed friends. They may have tried to give me flak, but I was, whatever. I'm not known for listening to people when they try to say bad stuff about me. Screw you. I don't *have* to hang out with you. They probably thought I was crazy, anyway.

It wasn't until eighth grade that any significant changes set in. I started to not be oblivious. I started thinking—really thinking about the world around me. I went through an ultra fem phase. I had hair down to my belly button—long and straight. It was nice hair, so I just wore it down. Sometimes I tucked it behind my ears.

Then I had a tomboy phase in which I would braid my hair back and keep it out of my face. I had a short goth phase, where I'd wear a lot of black, heavy eyeliner. That was fun.

And then, that April, I cut my hair. I went from belly button–length hair to a pixie cut. I was so happy that day. I said, "Whoa, this is awesome. This is something new." It looked awesome.

The reason I got my haircut was not because I wanted to look like a boy. During spring break I went to Florida to visit my grandma. I would go into the ocean and then spend half an hour in the shower with conditioner trying to untangle my hair. After that I was, "I am done with this mess. It needs to go!" So when I got back home, I got a pixie cut. It was pretty cool.

By this point, even I would have thought I was crazy. Not just with the hair. I was a weird kid.

My name came from one of those phases. I came up with a bunch of names to represent different parts of me because the name that I had been given wasn't going to cover it. The name I chose to work with was Cameron — for tomboy me. So when tomboy-me became boy-me, I became Cameron.

I knew that I wanted a middle name that would work with my first name, but I had time to make that decision. At hippie camp, an academic summer camp at Skidmore College, there was a plaza that people had paid to put names on. And *Joel La Plume* was one of the names. "Joel?" Aha! Middle name!

It's not, like, naming myself after Billy Joel or anything. It doesn't have any significance. I almost wish that *Joel* was my first name because it's a really cool name, but, like, whatever.

People who aren't trans get stuck with names all the time and it's not even that I don't like Cameron. I love it. It's gender neutral. It's perfect.

A name doesn't have to be perfect. A name isn't even who you are. It's like a variable in math. You call a number x. But x doesn't determine what the number is. It's something to refer to for a particular unknown, x. So my particular set of complex personality traits, and all that mush, is Cameron.

Most people go through traumatic stories about puberty, about how they hated it. Me? Not so much. I was happy when my breasts started growing. It was, like, whoa . . . my chest doesn't go like this anymore when I look down at it. Whoa, it's not a straight line anymore. It actually goes like this.

Cameron moves their hand up and down in a series of curves.

Whatever. I don't have body issues. My body is a pretty nice one. It works.

Coming Out Trans

My coming out trans story is kind of interesting. I was back at hippie camp. It was the summer after eighth grade. I was fourteen. I wasn't too good at scheduling things back then, but I did know that after hippie camp, I'd spend two weeks at home, and then the whole family would go on vacation at the Jersey shore. I planned to come out during the two weeks at home.

There was a change of plans. We weren't going to be home for two weeks; we were going to be home for one week. That wasn't enough time to come out, get new clothes, and try to, like, not be a girl.

I had no clue what I was doing. I thought, *I can't do this.* I debated whether I should stay in camp, change my coming-out schedule, or do something else. I couldn't focus on the classes I was taking. My doodles were about being trans.

I talked to the camp director and told her I was trans. I didn't want her to tell my parents because I needed to do that myself.

The camp director called my parents and said I needed to come home early but wouldn't tell them why. That must have gotten them thinking.

My dad picked me up August 3, 2009, just before I started high school. Everything was fine as we drove home together. Then, out of the blue, he said, "Do you want an operation to change your sex?"

And I was, like, "Oh shit, oh shit, oh shit." I bit my lip and didn't say anything.

Even if I had thought about surgery, I was not about to say, "No, I really don't want it," 'cause dad was not yet at a place where he could understand what *I* meant by trans.

Being trans is not something that is accurately portrayed in the media. So even if my dad had seen stories in the news, they would not have included trans theory; they would not be all encompassing. And since there are so many ways to be trans, and so much diversity within the trans community, he wouldn't have any idea about who I was. No. Anything about me had to be communicated by me. And that would take time.

I've always been pretty decent about trying to explain things. They did their Internet research and I tried to answer their questions in a nonthreatening, non-alienating way. I tried to help my parents understand how much more comfortable hormones will make me. It really is a comfort thing. I emphasized that hormones will help with all the awkward moments in public when people misgender me. I don't remember if I explained that to them exactly like that, but it was definitely a selling point.

The Plan

I don't remember even thinking about an operation back then. At that point, I thought that I'd come out, then get new clothes, and then start high school as Cameron—a boy.

After that, I wanted hormones and top surgery. I didn't want bottom surgery because the options aren't that great and it's really not something I need. Like I said, I don't have body issues. I'm not dysphoric.

> *Cameron's parents went with them to consultations and talked with the doctor. They wanted assurances that hormone therapy would be safe. There were times when Cameron got agitated, annoyed, teary, irritated, and upset. But everyone hung in. "The point of being parents is they care about you," they explained.*
>
> *When the hormone therapy was set up and ready to go, Cameron's mother went with them for their first hormone shot. Their dad would have gone too, but he was working.*

A week before I started high school, my mom and I talked with the principal and with the social worker. My mom was worried about name calling and harassment. "Mom, it's going to be okay," I told her. I was right. But if my parents weren't supporting me, most of the teachers wouldn't have listened to me. My parents did support me, and the teachers listened.

The principal may have listened without my parents talking to him because he's awesome. Mr. Mandel is the principal at Ossining High School and is the best principal ever. Mr. Mandel didn't shy away from controversy or a dialogue the way a standard high-school principal might. A decade ago, when the current GSA (Gay-Straight Alliance) advisor wanted to form the group, Mr. Mandel said, "Great idea. Yes, we should definitely do this." Awesome.

The first day of high school was the day I came out to most of my friends. I put on a horrible-fitting polo shirt and shorts that were too big for me. I went to school and told people that I was a boy and my name is Cameron and to call me *he.*

They were, like, "What?"

"I'm a boy, and my name is Cameron, and call me *he.* I'm trans, transgender."

"Um, like, okay."

For the most part, they did.

I had some issues with two teachers, that didn't make a whole lot of sense to me 'cause they never knew me as a girl, so why would they call me *she?*

The thing with pronouns is, I can understand if people have trouble switching the pronouns if they have difficulty calling someone *he* when they called said person *she* for most of said person's life. But when someone who you've not met is told what pronouns to use, or if someone on your behalf tells them what pronouns to use, and it's totally disregarded, I don't think that's okay.

Names too. I never had issues with my name. For some reason nouns are easier to remember than pronouns.

I confronted those teachers indirectly because the social worker at the school was on my side. "Well, this teacher was not listening to me when I said call me *he.*" And the social worker talked to the teacher.

But if I had confronted the teachers and been aggressive about it, they probably would have said, "Oh, I'm sorry, you look like a girl to me." *That* would not have been okay. A, because it's just rude to tell a trans guy he looks like a girl for obvious reasons—because in many cases that's what he's trying not to look like. And B, that's no excuse to disregard pronouns just because somebody looks like something else. That's stupid. Yeah.

. . .

Overall, the environment for gay kids at OHS is pretty awesome. I'm about as queer as you can get, and I didn't get crap from anyone. I'm currently president of the GSA and Noah is vice president. We're going to the gay prom together as friends.

I got one prank phone call: "I'm looking for the gay."

Cameron mimics the call, using a deep, husky voice.

But I don't count that because it didn't really bother me, and it was only once. I'm as out as one can possibly be, and I'm getting away with only a prank phone call? Yes! Yes, please. That's awesome.

I didn't go through any kind of harassment, which was kind of weird. Most of the trans people I know go through some situation or some story about being bullied or harassed. I didn't have that. I had a strong support system in place.

Without New York City or New Haven nearby, there would be no therapy, no testosterone, no trans kids or parents of trans kids support groups. If I didn't live in Westchester, there would be no gay prom, no PFLAG (Parents, Families, and Friends of Lesbians and Gays) group for my parents.

I think the lack of crap I've gotten about being trans and queer and all that has enabled me to be stronger. I wanted to make sure I took advantage of that in the future. I wanted to make use of my strength by helping others.

There is a course offered called "Gender Ideology." It is half women's studies and half queer theory. I'm taking it, of course, and it's going to be awesome. We do have other controversial classes. There's a class called "Racism, Classism, and Sexism." It was given at the high school, but it's a university class from SUNY, Albany. I took it and it was pretty phenomenal.

Hormones

November 11, 2010. A month before I turned sixteen, I began taking hormones. That's why my voice is low.

November 11, 2011 was one year on T (testosterone), which is pretty cool.

My period stopped two months after I started T. My voice started dropping a little before Christmas. There was some shrinkage in my breasts, which was cool. I started shaving. I can feel some stubble right now. My mustache grows fastest.

Testosterone is definitely a sexy hormone. My sex drive went way up once I started taking it. Testosterone makes me go *Kajooo! Kajooo! Kajooo!* What's really weird and kind of bizarre is that my testosterone level fluctuates. A couple of days after the shot, the level is at the highest, and a couple of days before the shot it is at the lowest. My sex drive fluctuates too. Right after the shot I'm really horny, and before the shot I'm not good for anything.

I've been thinking about switching to a half a dose every week rather than a full dose every other week. It would be the same dose but less fluctuation. That would be good 'cause hormone fluctuations are not fun. It's not just sex. It's the mood swings and the energy swings. My mood goes down before I get a shot. I'm like, blah, lethargic, and I get sort of moody.

There's a lot of information on side effects of testosterone. There's tons of legitimate information online. It's important to find information that really is legit.

Right now I'm sort of a lump, with no defined muscles. But if I actually do stuff like push-ups, my arms respond to that. It doesn't just happen overnight, but it's easier to build muscle. Hopefully I will be doing that this summer.

Male Privilege

Because I'm perceived as male, I get male privileges. It weirds me out a little bit. Male privilege means I don't have to prove myself for my opinion to have weight. People assume that I'm intelligent. People assume that I have something to say. I get a fair amount of respect.

By being male, I'm automatically given some kind of validity that is weird. "Wait, guys, I haven't said anything yet. And besides, you shouldn't be giving me male privilege because I'm not really a guy—at least not by your standards. By your standards, I'm definitely not."

People don't see me as a person they can talk down to. A stranger won't call me "sweetheart." The only person who can call me "sweetheart" is my grandma.

I like to think that I can fend off society's male expectations pretty well. Society wants all kinds of things from the boys. They want us to be masculine and to wrestle, to swear, and to be aggressive and assertive. To some degree, society wants us to be misogynistic. But I've never really gone along with what people say I should do, in case you didn't notice. I do more things to actively *not* fit male expectations than I do to fit the expectations.

I'm wearing five earrings—I got that done yesterday. Five earrings is a minor act of rebellion at society and gender 'cause guys are supposed to wear one earring, if any. However minor that may be, it's something I'm supposed to be doing, so I don't do it.

Sewing is not something I'm supposed to be doing, either. I tailored this shirt because it was too big for me. I like it a lot better. It was not flattering before; it was like a bag.

And another thing is guys are not supposed to wear bright colors. The standard colors of guys are basically limited to gray, black, brown, dark green, dark blue, maybe dark maroon, white, sometimes orange, but that's about it. And I'm like, nope, I'm not going to do that. I'll go with purple.

Whenever I wear a tie, it's almost always colorful. The most beautiful tie I ever had was hot pink. But I also have a skinny, rainbow tie that's awesome too.

Now, About My Brother

I first came out to my brother back at hippie camp, which happened right before nerd camp. At this hippie camp, everyone was different and way more awesome than they are in the real world, myself included. When I first came out to my brother, he was really cool about it. But when we got back to the real world, and it was time for middle school again, he stopped being cool about it. At first he would use pronouns as a weapon. Whenever he was mad at me, he'd call me *she,* and whenever he wasn't mad at me, he'd call me *he.* And when he was really pissed, I was *that thing.*

I think that was just a basic sibling rivalry thing, I don't think it was because I came out. You're pissed at your sibling, you're not going to give them human status. It's "that thing across the dinner table."

The first few times he said it, I was chill, but after a while I started picking up a trend that happened whenever he got mad. I became pretty pissed because that is *not* playing fair, that is hitting way below the belt, and it is not acceptable. I tried to confront him, but that didn't work out because my brother is far more aggressive than I am, far more confrontational than I am. He can out-confront me. At this point, he doesn't want to talk about anything trans or queer related, and that's kind of difficult. He's into cycling, he's a hard-core cyclist, and he talks about that with Dad 24/7. And I barely ever talk about trans things, or at least barely ever in relation to how much he talks about cycling. Whenever I bring it up, he says, "We always talk about trans stuff."

"Nope. Not really. We always talk about cycling. Shut up."

We're expected to fight. We're teenage brothers, so that's just how it goes.

For the most part, his old friends know that I'm trans and call me *he*. I don't hang out with the new friends he has because they're annoying.

We're fourteen and a half months apart, but we're two years apart in school because I'm like a junior, rising senior. It's very exciting. That means I have to apply to college.

I think we will get better when I leave for college because I won't have to deal with him on a daily basis, and he and my parents won't have to deal with me on a daily basis.

My understanding is that people at school ask him questions about me instead of asking me, which is really, really weird. It's like, "If you talk to Cam, you're going to catch the trans? You can't talk to Cam!" I don't know. People are silly about that.

Once I don't have to deal with him every day, and share a bathroom with him, and have to see him being a slob every day, then, yeah, we'll probably get closer.

Stand Together

What's interesting is that the straight, non-trans population seems to think that trans people automatically have allies in gay people. And that gay people automatically have allies in the trans community. And they do Not, capital *N*.

We need to stand together to fight the system. If trans people stand alone, we have no chance. *No chance at all!* I think all people who are oppressed in one way or another should stand together—women, queer people, people of color, disabled people, whatever. All the special-interest groups, minority groups, have a much better chance of effecting change if we stick together. We definitely shouldn't hate each other. That's a stupid thing.

Life goal: be part of the revolution! It's on my bucket list—I don't have a bucket list, but if I did, revolution would be on it. High up! Definitely high up!

I want to be a doctor. I will find a queer organization and work with queer kids and prescribe hormones to trans kids. It's going to be cool.

We have so much potential. Together we have the potential for dynamic change. A revolution. I hope a revolution happens. And I want to be in it.

I think *potential* is a good thing to end on because it's happy. It's about the future. I'm looking forward to my future. I've done a lot of thinking about it, and not just the big stuff, little things too. Having a driver's license. Turning twenty-one. Going to college. Making new friends.

Who I meet in college will have a huge effect on who I am and what I do and how I interact with the world. Will I really end up going to med school? Where will I live? What will my world be like? There's no way to predict what's going to happen. I guess that's the thing I'm actively trying to do—not predict what's going to happen.

Life's an adventure. It really is an adventure.

NAT

Something Else

How can I explain myself to someone normal? I'm hard to explain. Usually I don't like to use labels, but if I did, I would say I was gender queer, gender neutral, or simply queer. Intersex is another way I can identify myself. Intersex means that I'm both male and female. It means I'm neither male nor female; I'm a whole different gender, a third gender, so to speak, part of the transgender umbrella.

> *Intersex people can be identified a number of ways: by their genitalia, by secondary sex characteristics, or by chromosomes. They can be physically both male and female. Or they can externally look like one sex but internally be another sex.*

My birth certificate says I'm female. I guess I looked female when I was born. I thought you follow whatever's on your birth certificate. But maybe that isn't always true.

Everyone always said I was weird, so that's how I considered myself. That's 'cause I was called a freak in middle school. And weird. A weird freak!

I was taller and broader than most girls. I looked like a girl—but not exactly like a girl. I acted like a boy, but I wasn't a boy. When people became more sexual, around eighth grade, everyone assumed I was gay or lesbian.

I want people to use the pronouns *them* and *they* when referring to me because I consider myself both male and female. Since most people don't understand that, I just tell them to use *he*. For years I was *she*, so it's time to switch. I don't like being a girl. I gave it a run. It didn't work.

This chapter refers to Nat as them *or* they.

I never wanted to be a pretty girl, or even a pretty girl with a touch of boy. I thought of myself as just a kid. I'd sleep, eat breakfast, and go to school, draw something on the chalkboard, go back home, eat, sleep, and repeat. I never thought, *Oh, I'm pretty today,* or *Oh, I want to look like a boy today.* I don't recall anything like that.

I had an image in my head about how my body's supposed to look. I wanted to look androgynous, in between, as if you can't tell that I have male or female genitalia. It's a nice image. When people say I look male or female, it messes up my head.

The long road with musical interludes

In the Beginning

I was born in New York City. My mom is Italian and French, and my dad is German, some other European nationality, and some indigenous tribe in Chile. But both are from Chile. At home, we speak English and Spanish.

According to my parents, it took four years to have me because they didn't really like each other. They were fighting a lot. They said that those four years were living hell. My mom was forced to marry my father by her mother, my grandmother. My grandmother met my father, thought he was a good, decent guy, and said, "Oh, you should meet my daughter and marry her." They married, spent four years in hell, and then they had me. A year later, they had my brother, Jova. I think he's straight because he's totally homophobic.

Even though my dad worked, my mom complained that he didn't do anything. I don't know what he does to this day. Me and my father don't talk that much. He has worked the same job forever. My mom used to work, but after she had me, she stopped.

My parents told me that I didn't speak until I was seven. As a kid, I didn't speak at all. Most of the time, I just pointed. I started making sounds when I was around six or five. My guess is it was because the two languages confused me. I was going to a school where everyone spoke English. My dad said we had to speak English at home, not only to improve me but also to improve my parents' English.

They loved speaking English. The problem was my grandmother never learned the language. One moment they spoke English; the next moment they had to speak Spanish.

Before preschool I did everything in my house. I was always alone. Even with my brother living in the same house, in the same room, I was a solitary kid. I used my imagination a lot. I thought of my toys as a way to see what I was thinking. Let's say I had a movie in my head and wanted to see it visually. I guess when you're a kid you need to see things visually. You need to know it's real. Like, to pretend two knights fighting, I'd use two dolls or two action figures to enact what I had imagined. But I wasn't comfortable doing that in front of people. I needed to be alone to do that.

I didn't like preschool, but I felt good about being five. Five is my favorite number because it reminds me of the time when I wasn't forced to think of myself as a girl or a boy. I was neutral. I didn't have to explain myself. I wasn't depressed. I never got into fights and I never had arguments with my family. I could go into my room and play with my toys and no one bothered me. Is it normal for a kid to do that? I don't know.

There's a major difference between being in your room playing with your toys and being in a room full of kids and playing with your toys. In preschool, like, if I had a toy, other kids might try to take it away from me. For me, that was an invasion of my privacy.

I had short hair, and my mom dressed me in shirts and pants. When I think about myself back then, I looked neutral. Sometimes I had a sweater with a horse on it. I don't remember wearing pink or bows in my hair—maybe I did when I was a baby, but that doesn't matter.

Then, later on, when they started separating kids according to sex, that really started to bug me. I got in trouble a lot. One time, when I was six, I was playing basketball with the guys in the school yard. We were in two teams, the shirts versus the skins. I was in the skins. So when all the guys took their shirts off, I took my shirt off too. I didn't think anything of it. One of the recess guards pulled me away and yelled at me. I didn't know what happened. By the end of the school day, my teacher was talking to my mother. My mother dragged me all the way back to our apartment, all the while saying mean things to me. I think she hit me twice. I just remember her screaming at me, and she said it in Spanish, which I personally believe hurts even more than when it is said in English.

"*¿Por qué haces esto a mí?*" (Why do you do this to me?) "*No hacer cosas estúpidas.*" (Don't do stupid things.) "*La gente va a pensar que tu eres rara.*" (People will think you are weird.)

I felt terrible. Then my dad came home, and obviously my mom told him, because he screamed at me too. All that just because I took my shirt off? I didn't know I shouldn't!

I guess when you're born a girl people assume you know that you're a girl. Period! My parents bought me Barbie dolls and my brother action figures. I liked them both—I really did. One side of me wanted the Barbies, but the other side wanted the action figures. Because I couldn't play with action figures, I took off the heads of my Barbie dolls. I pulled them apart.

I liked them both, and they forced me to one side, like, I had to only play with dolls.

I never talked about my feelings, even when I was a kid. It's not that I didn't trust my family. It's just I didn't feel comfortable talking to them about anything. It was a gut feeling. I mean, I'd say "hi" to my mom, and I'd say, "I love you," because that's what she expected to hear. I respected her. She's a nice woman. We had some tough times together that I'll tell you about, but she's not completely bad. There are times when I mean it when I say, "I love you," and there are times when I say it because she wants to hear it.

At this point in Nat's life, they were referred to as she. *Their family thought that once they began preschool, they would start speaking. But they didn't. From kindergarten to second grade, Nat was in special ed.*

Special

Special ed. was nice because there were just eight kids in the class. I was the only girl. Everyone was there for a reason. One kid didn't think fast. Another had temper tantrums. I had problems connecting with people because I had a speech problem, I couldn't exactly express how I felt. I knew what I wanted to say, but because I lacked the vocabulary, I couldn't give a complete message. People would brush me away and say I was being silly.

Bathrooms became a big issue for me. First of all, they weren't the cleanest places in the world. Also, I just assumed you can go into any bathroom. But the teachers told me I had to go to the girls' bathroom. If I went into the boys' bathroom by accident, the teacher would pull me out. I didn't understand. All the bathrooms looked the same to me. So I was, like, "You know what? I'm not going to any bathroom because that's too confusing." I would literally hold whatever I had for the whole day until I went home.

I developed a urinary problem that lasted till fifth grade. I didn't wet my bed; I wet my pants in school. If I was embarrassed, if I felt I wasn't understood, or if I was sad, I'd wet my pants. Then I'd be even more embarrassed, misunderstood, and sad. If I did it early I would have to go through the entire day with wet pants. I tried to hide it, but people weren't that stupid. It's embarrassing to admit this.

In third grade, I was put in a regular classroom, but in the same school. I went from classes with eight kids to classes with about thirty. All of a sudden, I was forced to wear a skirt and panty hose. I hated it. Panty hose! I hated it completely. I liked to run around, and I'd fall and rip my panty hose. My mom would get mad because she had to pay for new ones.

My hair grew long, and my mother pulled it tight into a ponytail. That hurt so much, I felt like my head was stretching.

I felt weird because I still couldn't express myself. In my head, I didn't feel like a girl; I felt more like a boy. But I didn't identify myself as a boy, either. I started reading lots of books about stuff considered androgynous or hermaphroditic, and I looked at a lot of pictures. I learned that there are people who look like both sexes but are not both sexes. They're another gender—a third gender. You know how during the Renaissance the portraits seem androgynous? I was attracted to that.

Sex and human anatomy were not something talked about in my traditional, Roman Catholic family. When I was around twelve or thirteen, my mom gave me hints, like, "A woman has an egg." I thought, *What's that? What's the point of that? Why is everyone so obsessed with this?* So I thought I had better find out. I didn't want to talk about it with friends because you don't know who's going to be a tattletale. And the last thing I wanted to be was in trouble. I looked it up in my dad's encyclopedia and saw the egg and the sperm, and back and forth. I needed to know more, so I went to the library. I wouldn't go straight to the books about sex because a thirteen-year-old looking at those kinds of books, asking for those kinds of books, might make the librarian look at me a little suspicious. When I finally found out what sex was about, I said to myself, *Okay, that's like, whatever.*

So Girly

Girls were becoming problematic for me. They were so girly. And they were so gossipy. They talked about things I never understood. It's not like I was stupid, I just wasn't interested. Clothes. Making fun of boys. Stuff about TV shows or the newest toys. They wanted to make a secret girls' club, and I'm, like, "What the hell is this?" I never got into it.

Also, if you do one bad thing to a girl, and she has a group, the whole group will give you the cold shoulder and treat you like crap for God knows how long.

I tried to make friends with them, but little things hurt me. Like, once we went on a trip and a girl promised to be my partner. I don't want to say her name, but this girl said she'd be my friend and we'd be friends forever. At the last minute she decided to partner with someone else. She left me, just like that. This happened a bunch of times.

The girls called me weird because I didn't get the stuff they talked about. I knew I was smarter than they were, but when they gossiped or talked about girly stuff, I'd say, "What are you talking about? That's stupid!" I'd say to them.

Once, one of the girls said, "Oh, the teacher thinks I'm stupid."

I said, "That's because you don't talk about educational stuff. You talk about sex and some other crap. You don't even speak English well."

I guess I was a little too outspoken, especially since I was the one with the speech problem. That must have hurt her because her clique gave me the cold shoulder afterward.

Although Nat was confident of their intellectual capabilities, they continued to have speech problems and could not express themself clearly. People began to think Nat was slow. They weren't.

Nat was physically stronger than the other girls. But because they were considered female, and because in Nat's world, females were stereotyped as weak, they did not have the opportunity to show how strong they were. Basically, society would not let Nat be Nat.

Yeah, that's exactly right. By the fifth grade, I thought, *You know what? I'm graduating to middle school and will never see you people again.* Middle school was in a new building. A new school! A new environment! I couldn't wait to be rid of those girls.

Middle-School Crap

If elementary school was about making fun of boys, middle school was about being attracted to boys. To make matters worse, half the people in my new school were the very ones I hated in elementary school. Crap! *That* group? Three more years with them? Crap!

My mother said, "It's a new school and a new year. Leave everything behind you. You're there to be educated." I took her advice and I tried. I really tried hard. I thought my life would become better if I just studied and stayed away from the girls, but it actually became worse.

Sexual stuff was starting to happen. Girls would blow kisses to guys and say, "Oh, you're so cute," this and that. Whatever. And guys would say, "Oh, you're so pretty."

I was sitting there thinking, *I don't understand any of this.* I felt left out too, because no one ever said that to me. I didn't feel exactly pretty or attractive. My mom said I was pretty, but I'm her kid. Parents always find their kids beautiful. But I didn't look like most girls. I looked like something else. I went through a lot of teasing because of this. Most girls my age are slim and have curves. Not me.

Everyone said I wasn't fat, but compared to the other girls, I would say I was fat. The other girls were really, really skinny. I called them sticks. That's how skinny they were.

From first to sixth grade, my mom chose all my clothes. Once I reached middle school, I wanted to pick my own clothes. "I know how to take care of myself," I told her. "Everyone is choosing their own clothes. As long as I'm not showing any skin, like any slut out there, I think I can do it." She had to agree. We lived in a neighborhood where there were a lot of slutty-type girls. I don't think they were actual sluts, but that's the way they dressed.

I mostly wore neutral clothes, like a shirt and gray pants. I always kept a sweater on. Even if it was eighty degrees outside, I would keep my sweater on all day. I didn't like to show my body. I didn't like the way I looked. People said I looked physically weird, and I believed them.

I never looked at myself in the mirror. The moment I looked in the mirror, I would get depressed for a month. That's how extreme it was.

My mom wouldn't let me cut my hair, even though I hated the way it looked. It got longer and longer, so I put it up in a bun.

I liked school for the education but I didn't like the social atmosphere. I took art and music. I love those types of things. And I loved to read. But being with other kids, studying with other kids, interacting with kids my own age? I didn't like that. I didn't know how to interact with people, and that was a problem.

I did manage to have one group of friends—three guys and a girl. The girl became my friend last because I didn't want to hang out with females. But she seemed nice, and she was tomboyish, so okay, I was cool with it.

The three guys were, like, outcasts, nerdy people. You have your cool kids and you have the nerds. I interacted with the nerds mostly. I sat next to one of the guys in math class. During a test, I didn't know an answer, and he helped me.

I know, that's cheating, but it was very nice of him. We started talking, and he introduced me to the two other guys. Then once, during study hour, there were no seats except for one next to this girl. So I sat down. She was a nerd girl too, because she was drawing cartoons and stuff. I didn't want to be the kind of person who hated all girls, even though in my experiences most of them weren't great. We started talking, and I thought she's not that bad. We're still in contact. It's really ironic because I no longer see the guys.

Until late middle school, me and my brother shared a room. My dad said I needed my privacy. I never asked for privacy. "I don't need privacy," I told him. "I'm good for having someone to share a bedroom with." But my dad insisted, and that isolated me more. By seventh and eighth grade, I was really angry. I went from "quiet" to "pissed off."

Around this time, I began to grow breasts. They wouldn't be considered breasts in the normal sense; it was more like fat. You know how when fat guys have . . .

Nat holds their hands up as if they're holding two large melons.

It was like that.

I started to notice that my body was changing. But I wasn't developing like girls. When I tried to compare myself to boys, I wasn't like them, either. So where the hell should I go? I had a lot of trouble losing weight. I tried to lose weight for years and never lost a pound. I don't want to sound like a victim, or whatever, but I constantly asked myself, "What am I?"

Fame

LaGuardia High School is a specialized school. It's famous for music and art, and it's just across the street from Lincoln Center. To give a general idea of the school, you know the movie *Fame? Fame* is based on LaGuardia. To get in, you have to take a test and do an audition. I think I'm smart, but I'm a terrible test taker. I auditioned for both music and art, but only got into art. I was doing fantasy art, abstract drawings.

At first I was pretty happy there. I had finally gotten rid of those awful middle-school girls. It was, like, "Good-bye I'm never going to see you again!" I tried to wear pretty shirts and stuff. I didn't wear a dress, but I had nice pants, jeans. I tried to make my mom happy and just give "girl" a try. To tell you the truth, I wasn't comfortable with this, so I went back to wearing neutral clothing—and back to feeling confused.

I wanted to study music too and thought, *Hey, I got in for art—I'll figure out how to get into the music part later*. I told the music-school director that I played the violin and wanted to take classes. I played the violin, but I started at twelve, instead of the typical five, six, or seven. I said, "If I can't play violin, put me in any beginner instrumental class." Because I majored in art, the director told me that was impossible.

Every day I went to the office and asked to be put in a music class. I did that for a whole year. By my sophomore year, the director said, "Oh, you're that person again? We'll just give you it." I went to a winds class and took tenor saxophone. It wasn't the violin but, hey, it was a start.

I was getting 90s in winds and decided to push it a little further. I talked to my band teachers and asked about a teacher for strings. They recommended Dr. Washington, a very tough teacher. The tough teachers are the best.

She was the only strings teacher who asked me to audition. When I auditioned, I made a few mistakes, but I tried my best. She said, "I'll put you in my orchestra." So I was in her orchestra and her strings class. I was in Orchestra 6 and worked my way up to Orchestra 7, the second best orchestra in the school.

That was hard because I was taking both art and music classes. My school days doubled. I didn't mind the long hours and hard work, but I was not comfortable with the student body. High school is a tough time when it comes to teasing, bullying.

"Even in an art school?" I ask. One would think that music and art students would be more open-minded.

I know—that's what I say. You would think that they would understand me 'cause art people are supposed to be open. But everyone was very competitive. Everyone was against each other, trying to get their art displayed in the gallery. Some people would write that off as competition. I saw it as bullying. And in the music classes, to tell you the truth, I didn't get a lot of respect. Most kids started playing early. They took lessons with private teachers. My family couldn't afford that. One student violinist told me, "I've been playing for eight or nine years."

"I've been playing for three or four."

"How in the world did you get into this orchestra?"

"Because I just got in."

Everything was getting really sexual in high school. Kids were saying, "Oh, having sex is great. I feel like having sex." And I'm, like, I don't feel anything. I was attracted to some people but not to the point where I would want to go to bed with them. Sex is still not high on my list.

Not only did the talk become sexual, but also girls were dressing in more revealing clothes. Even the guys tried to reveal more of their bodies. And I became more and more uncomfortable. I thought of myself as a mix of feminine and masculine, leaning more toward the masculine side. I said to myself, *I think of myself as a guy. But I don't identify as a boy completely. So how in the world can I explain this?* It was confusing. It was confusing to say I'm neither gender.

I didn't talk to my parents about it because I knew they would never understand. Everybody is used to two sexes. I was already called a freak, and I didn't want to risk more. I started to learn about gay stuff, on my own. One time in my neighborhood, I saw one guy give another guy a kiss. What was that? It was so awesome, but I didn't know the name for it. That's when I learned more about gay stuff or LGBTQ stuff.

Inside/Outside

In my high school, we took special health classes to show us how our bodies were changing during puberty. I said to myself, *This is not how my body is changing.* Like, when a girl gets her period, that's supposed to come when she's around thirteen, fourteen. Right? Mine came when I was seventeen, and only once or twice. Also, I couldn't lose weight. That's when my mom took me to a series of endocrinologists to see what was going on.

I went to five different endocrinologists, three females and two males. The first doctor, a woman, checked my blood and gave me a physical examination. She gave me some kind of medication, but it didn't work out, so we went to a second endocrinologist. She recommended a sonogram. To take one, I had to drink a lot of water. It was painful. She checked my ovaries and couldn't figure out what was going on. They looked like ovaries, but they had an unusual white lining around them. She thought it might be testosterone.

The third doctor, male, gave me another sonogram. He said that I had PCOS (polycystic ovary syndrome). PCOS means that during my development in the womb, it wasn't clear whether I wanted testes or ovaries. That's how I understand it, but maybe a doctor will give you a better explanation. This third doctor said that I was a whole different gender. That diagnosis made perfect sense to me. In fact, it made me happy and relieved.

But it also created problems with my mother. After we left the doctor's office, she went into denial mode and said, "Oh that's a bunch of crap. You know how doctors are. They say this just to make themselves look smart."

The fourth doctor said I might have ova-testes—that's in between ovaries and testes.

The fifth one took all the information from the other doctors and said she agreed with PCOS, the third doctor. She said my ovaries didn't act

like ovaries. I was making more testosterone than estrogen. Males and females both have testosterone, but females only have a small amount of testosterone. As an assigned female, I was making way too much testosterone. She assumed I was a girl. She assumed I wanted to be a girl. So she gave me medication to bring down the testosterone down and boost up my estrogen.

Did Nat want this?

No! I didn't know what I wanted, but that was definitely *not* it.

When the doctors confirmed that I was intersex, I thought, *Wow, I'm that whole other gender!* It proved what I had been feeling all along. I was not only emotionally, psychologically, and spiritually both sexes; I was physically both sexes too. This is who I am.

My mom was still in denial. She kept asking why I didn't have a boyfriend.

Discoveries

In my sophomore year, I tried going to a GSA (Gay-Straight Alliance) meeting. It turned out to be mostly a hook-up scene. I thought the Gay-Straight Alliance would be gay people and straight people trying to understand each other. No. It was mostly gay people and people who say they're bisexual talking about sex. I saw it as complete bullshit. I was disappointed. I held my anger inside and pretended I was okay about school.

Meanwhile, my grandma forced us to go church every Sunday. I'm not saying I didn't like church, but if I didn't feel like going, why should I go? Not that I don't believe in God. But if there is a God, maybe I was supposed to be born this way. There has to be a reason. But what is it?

Nat was unable to come up with a reason that satisfied society or the church.

I felt that I was bringing bad energy to what people consider a holy place. So I stopped going to church.

During this period, I tried to be more open. People say high school is when you really discover yourself. I said to myself, *Let me give it a try.* I explained to people that I was a third gender. When I tried, most people thought that I didn't know what I was talking about. Or they thought of me as a joke. So I thought there was no point talking about this.

I began seeing a social worker my sophomore year. His name was John. He was a very nice guy. I explained how I felt, and he listened to me. I think it was hard for him to understand. To me, being a third gender makes perfect sense, but it doesn't make sense to other people.

That Kiss

Around my sophomore year, I bumped into one of my old middle-school friends. She wasn't actually a friend; I knew her because we sat next to each other in math class and she lived in my neighborhood. She had just broken up with her boyfriend, who I also knew, and she wanted to talk about it to me. She said I was a nice person to talk to because I was, like, nonbiased.

At that time, everyone saw me as a girl, and she did too. In a weird way, I understand both girls and guys—as much as I don't want to admit it. Anyway, she started to get into the sexual stuff. That didn't bother me. I thought, *She's just a teenager; she doesn't know what she's talking about.*

According to her, she was bisexual. One time she decided to kiss me. I thought, she's a human being and she just wanted some kind of physical affection. I was trying to be a friend. I didn't feel anything. I was just helping out a friend.

For some reason, she decided to tell her ex-boyfriend about the kiss. Then her ex-boyfriend decided to tell one of his friends. His friends had an Xbox. He went on a chat room and told people what he heard. One of the people in the chat room was my brother. Instead of going directly to me about it, my brother went directly to my parents.

That kiss didn't mean anything to me. I never saw it as a big deal. It was just kissing. I didn't want sex—that was the *last* thing I wanted. In a simple sense, it was a person helping another person through physical affection. That's how I viewed it, but other people viewed it as something different. They saw *Girl Kissing Girl*!

My parents called me into their room and said "We heard about this. Is it true?"

I automatically lied 'cause I knew they wouldn't approve. "That's a lie! People make shit up."

Then I called the girl, and I asked why she thought it was okay to talk about this. I asked her to please lie for me because I knew how my parents were. Then I called everyone who knew about this: her ex-boyfriend, her ex-boyfriend's friends, my brother, and my brother's friend. Eleven people. Nobody would lie for me. Here were people who said they were my friends but wouldn't lie for me.

My mom made me come to her room and stand in the corner. Then she brought each person in to tell her what happened. I had to watch and listen. As each one told her what he heard, I tried not to cry. I thought that was the strong thing to do. I had to hear this story eleven times. I was never given the chance to speak. My parents always said that they were my support system. But they didn't support me at all.

Finally, my mom said that what I did was wrong, that girls weren't supposed to kiss girls. I said, "You see what I don't see? I don't see myself as a girl."

As punishment, my computer and my cell phone were taken away. I had a strict curfew. When I finished school, I had to be home a half hour later. They thought the books I bought influenced how I acted, so they took them away from me.

I felt terrible. I didn't talk to anyone. I didn't feel that anyone understood me. I started to physically hurt myself. I started to cut. I heard that lots of people do this and it wasn't a big deal, so I tried to do even more. I started to burn myself.

Spiraling Down, Down, Down

I was always depressed, but by this point I got even more depressed. I stopped going to school. My brother and I weren't communicating. He was always home. I was always home. We stayed in separate rooms. My brother was fighting with my parents all the time. I guess you can say he had anger issues. One of his therapists called Child Services. They came to

the house every two weeks to check if we were eating well and this and that. According to this social worker, I was suffering from emotional neglect and my brother was suffering from educational neglect. It's a funny way to say it, but that's how they said it.

My mom wasn't very happy about this. When they came over and checked everything, she thought they treated her like a criminal, that she was not treating her kids well. She said, "You must think I'm a bad mother." I personally don't remember how we responded to that.

I thought, *Why am I depressed? I have everything good. I have a family. I have food. I have a house. I go to a good school.* I couldn't explain to Child Services why I was depressed. So I said to myself, *I'll just shut up because I'm just going to create more problems and no one's ever going to understand what I'm going through.*

Even though I had no desire to protect my family or anything like that, I just shut up and went along. I went with the flow, thinking, *Things will work out.*

Junior Year from Hell

I attempted suicide twice. The first time, I had a knife but I couldn't use it. I was really close to doing it, and I would have done it, but then something in my head said, *I would spill a lot of blood in the bathroom. And then my parents are going to yap at me even after I'm dead. That's another problem I don't need.* So I got myself out of it. But still, I felt unsatisfied.

The second time, I gave hints to my social worker that I wanted to do something. He called my parents, worried that something might happen.

The second time, when Nat was ready to attempt suicide, a phone call from the cousin of the "kiss girl" stopped them.

I still don't know why I picked up that phone. I guess it was an automatic reaction. The phone rings, you pick it up.

The social worker, John, wanted to send me to the hospital, and I kinda agreed with him. "I think I really need to go to the hospital," I told him.

To tell you the truth, as terrible as it sounds, that hospital gave me one of the best times of my life. I was still depressed, and I had to be on medication. But I was away from my parents. I was away from everyone. I wore hospital clothes, so people couldn't tell what sex I was.

The doctors did a physical examination. They said I had an abnormality on my genitalia because I had taken drugs or steroids. "I don't do drugs," I told them. "You can give me a tox screen. I don't do drugs or drink alcohol."

They sort of ignored that and said I have severe depression. At one point, they said I had a schizoid personality disorder. Those doctors weren't agreeing. And it wasn't just one doctor; it was a series of doctors. Each of them had a different opinion. From what I saw, they didn't communicate with each other much. It's like I got twenty different answers every day.

I made friends with two people. There was a girl in the emergency room. She said, "You don't look so well."

"I'm depressed."

"I cannot tell what you are," she said.

"I guess you can say that I'm queer."

"Oh, that's cool, because I'm a dyke."

That made me laugh.

The other person I made friends with was this guy named Thomas. He was a lot older than me. But I don't mind talking to older people. We talked about intellectual stuff, the arts. It was very cool. He used to be a doctor, and now he was a patient in the ward.

There were kids there too. Girls with eating disorders, guys with anger issues, teenagers with cutting problems. I was simply the weird one.

Sometimes my parents visited. I didn't want them there. I didn't want to think about the outside world where no one would ever understand who I was. My father still believed I was just going through a phase, teenage mood swings that got extreme for some reason. He never tried to understand.

My mom was disappointed. She never imagined that her kids would be in this type of situation. I guess when stuff like this happens, parents ask, "What did we do wrong?" I don't think it had anything to do with them.

After a month, I got out. It was May, near the end of the school year, so I decided not to go back to school. I didn't flunk out per se, but I had to make up the year.

Surprisingly, Nat felt more terrible once they left the hospital.

I fell into a deeper depression, and in August I went back to the hospital. This time I was diagnosed gender dysphoria. I think that's how they diagnose transgender people. Transsexuals. It's like, if you're physically one hundred percent one sex but you think you're the other sex, then you have this.

I continued to research "intersex" in the limited access I had to the hospital library. That's when I learned about hormone therapy. I considered myself gender queer intersex, but I thought hormones would get me closer to my ideal self. It's very difficult to explain. I mean, although I was both male and female, people still saw me as female. Maybe it was because I had breasts or my voice wasn't masculine enough. I just wanted people to accept me as me. I thought that hormone therapy would help me become my ideal self.

Nat's ideal self is hard to explain without invading their privacy. Suffice it to say, the hormones are working and Nat is coming closer to finding happiness.

Before I could get male hormones, I had to go to therapy sessions. I had to explain everything about myself. Even today, right here, I struggle talking about how I feel. I'm trying to be comfortable about myself. Now I'm getting ahead of myself.

I didn't want to go to school, but I forced myself just to get that diploma. I was still playing in the orchestra. I enjoyed that, but the other students didn't consider me a musician. I FYed everyone.

I was exhausted.

My average was 70 compared to when I started with a 93. But I graduated, and that's it.

I didn't want to go to graduation, but I had to. My mom and her friend were there. My dad was at my brother's graduation, which was held that morning, and then he came over to mine. After my name was called, he left. I was pissed.

After graduation, I heard my mom fighting with him on the phone. He didn't stay because he wanted to go back home and watch a soccer game between Argentina and Chile. If you're supposed to be a parent, you're supposed to be there for the whole graduation and not just leave for a stupid soccer game. This is not being a parent. This is not being a father. So I'm pissed. I did a lot of things to respect him, but he didn't do this one thing for his kid.

Moving Out

Because of my high-school grades, I only got into one college, in the CUNY system in Queens. So I went there.

I was fighting with my brother all the time. He always thought he was better than me. We were living under the same roof, but we weren't talking to each other.

On New Year's Day, my brother started throwing stuff at me. I told him to stop, and he wouldn't. We physically fought. My mom tried to separate us. He was yelling that he wasn't the one with the problem. "*She's* the one with the problem. *She's* the one that ruined the family because *she's* a freak."

Whenever the family called me *she,* I'd try to explain, "Please don't call me that. I'm not *she.*"

"No, that's what you are! *She!* End of story!" my brother said.

He said a lot of crap and called me hurtful things like faggot.

"That's it. I'm moving out."

I needed to get out of the environment that was making me feel bad about myself. I decided to live on my own. I now have my own apartment in Queens. It has a kitchen, a small bathroom; it's a studio basically.

Mindfulness

I talk to my mom a little bit more now, but I still keep her at arm's length. I don't talk with my father, and I don't talk with my brother at all.

I'm living on my own. My parents are separated, but not divorced because we are a strict, traditional Roman Catholic family. My mom's going to college and has a boyfriend. Dad lives with my brother; Mom lives with her mother. My mom's not fighting with my father as much. My brother is doing his own thing. My dad is doing his own thing. Not all families are perfect.

And me? Things are sort of going my way. I have my own place, I have a job, I'm taking hormone therapy, and I'm going to a support group at my clinic called "Mindfulness." I think it's to help get rid of negative thinking. I only went to one meeting so far and tomorrow is the second one. It doesn't hurt to try something new.

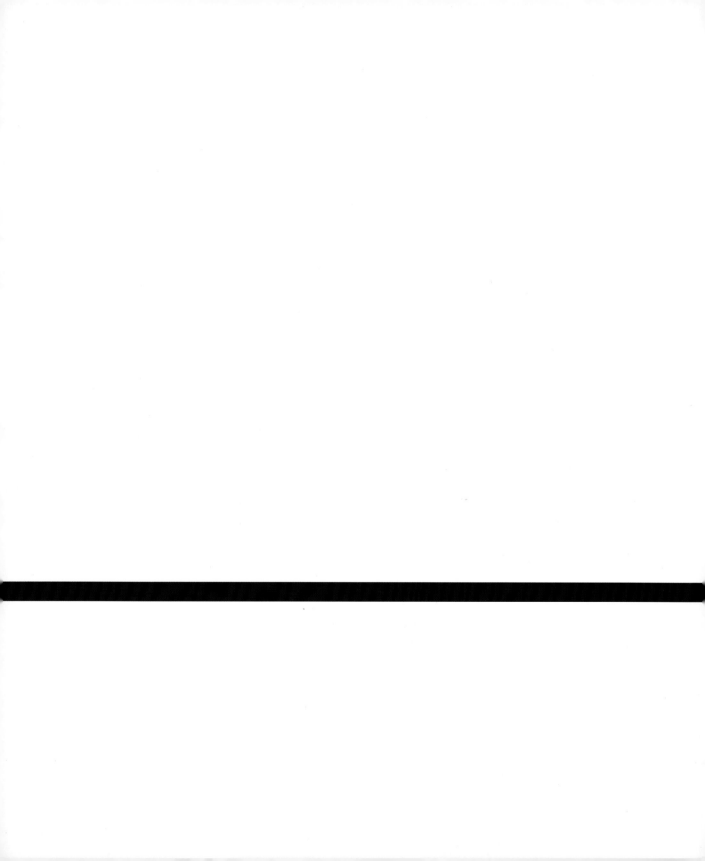

LIFELINE

LUKE
Untouchable

It's snowing in Madison, Wisconsin. Soft, sticky flakes slow down traffic and white out the majestic state capitol. Sixteen-year-old Luke (Luke's real name has been changed, and his image is only partially revealed, at the request of his family) is in rehearsal with an LBGTQ teen theater group called Proud Theater. Every week, teen actors and writers divide up into small groups to explore a chosen topic. They ask one another questions and share personal stories. Then they do improvisations, searching for common threads that could turn personal stories into something theatrical. At the end of the rehearsal, they all come together to present their theater pieces. The theme tonight is transgender youths.

On a bare stage with no lighting and three people in the audience, Luke rehearses a poem he wrote. Later in the evening, he will read it before the entire company.

They told me
> *No.*
Said, 'What are you?' said, 'you gotta choose'
> *said, 'Pink or blue?'*
and I said I'm a real nice color of
> *magenta*
> *everyday extremists that made this world just black*
> *And white solid stripes*
of a penitentiary uniform, imprisoned ourselves with nothing
but the ideas of who was on top and
> *who was on bottom,*
> *bathe yourself afterward,*
perhaps for the sake of hygiene, they told me, but gently
> *make sure that soap and water doesn't wash away your*
> *definition—*
> *red and sore down there from the moment those red curtains opened,*
> *exposing me to the cries of "It's a—"*
> *and*
> *fill*
> *in*
> *the*
> *blank*

on these paper pages, just wanna see how crazy you,
> *well not everything needs a diagnosis,*
> *and you blame it back on things past in childhood*
> *this is still my childhood*
professionally inferring that those hands down my pants
> *had wiped smooth like wet clay*
> *and re-sculpted something hideous.*
> *and they told me,*
> *hide it.*

But somewhere, there's this scared young woman in a black dress
on a claustrophobic staircase, bleeding

'cause that safety razor wasn't all that safe after all
backstage and illuminated by a blue ghost light, and she
finally dares to look you in the eye

Don't you dare look away.

> *And me*
> *and her*
> *we're gonna go dancing on air*
> *Filling the space between these canyon walls, our*
> *Bodies broken at the bottom.*
> *'Cause, yeah, you have to give up some things*
>   *to be*
> *untouchable.*

"WOO, WOO, WOO, WOW! Pow-er-ful! Powerful, man," shouts Sol Kelley-Jones, totally wrapped up in Luke's poetry. Sol, one of the founders of Proud Theater, is rehearsing Luke for an upcoming benefit performance that will be hosted by Chaz Bono. Luke is tall and lanky, with blue eyes and sandy-blond hair that flies here and there as he moves.

Slowly coming out of his impassioned, demanding poem, he looks to Sol, smiling. Luke is an accomplished actor, writer, and poet. He wrote the poem he just recited for a ninth-grade poetry slam at his school. At that time, he was the only out person in his school. "In middle school, nobody else was queer. It was great to be around people, theater people, that identified as queer, people whose company I enjoyed."

"Let's try it again," Sol says, after giving a few stage directions — when a turn becomes a pivot, when to look directly at the audience. Taking on the role of emcee, she shouts, "And now we have Proud Theater . . ."

"Yeah! Proud Theater!" Sol's also the audience. Clap! Clap! Clap! "Wooooo!"

Luke jumps up and down and shakes his long, tapered fingers like a whirlybird in preparation to recite again.

Watching Luke this evening, it is hard to imagine how shy he is offstage. Extreme shydom. Offstage he giggles lots. Onstage he's authoritative and in total control.

Luke performs the poem again.

"WHOA!" yells Sol before lowering her voice. "It's powerful stuff. Every time I hear it, I get new richness out of it. All right! Try it again."

Last year, when I started writing the poem, I knew I was trans but I didn't know if I was gender neutral or FTM (female-to-male). There's a lot you can say in poetry that you can't say in conversation. In poetry you can get images and you can get feelings. It's more abstract, but it's also more concrete.

I wanted to write a piece that I could do with authority. I wanted to explain this to my school. I wanted to explain it to myself too, because I didn't know who or what I was at that time. I got a very, very positive response, which I was proud of. The poem got a twenty-nine out of a thirty score, a pretty good rating.

At that time, I identified as female but presented in a masculine way. You've probably heard the expression "write what you know"? I wrote my poem when I was starting to think, *Maybe I'm trans, maybe I'm trans, maybe I'm trans,* and this is kinda given away in the first couple of lines.

> *Said, 'What are you?' said, 'you gotta choose'*
> *said, 'Pink or blue?'*
> *and I said I'm a real nice color of*
> *magenta*

Coming out trans is very exposing. It opens you up to a lot of mockery. The reason I wrote the poem as I did was to come out with a bang. I wrote it also to clear away some of the criticism that I knew would be coming. If you get up on a stage and say "I'm trans" by doing a poem—that is hopefully an all right poem—it is more impressive than just coming out. At least it was for me.

I wanted to perform it in the end-of-year Proud Theater program, but it was near showtime and I didn't push it. A couple of weeks ago, Brian (Brian Wild, the adult artistic director of the company) remembered it and asked me to do it for the benefit. I took it out and said to myself, *You know what? This sucks. I need to rewrite this.* So I did. I don't think I had it completely written down anywhere. It's all been memorized. Basically I wrote everything down as I remembered it and filled in the parts that I couldn't remember with stuff that I made up.

I'm not good about talking about poetry. I don't know how to do it. Poetry is like thoughts, it gets at things more accurately.

Luke's Life in Eight Scenes

Scene i: Proud Theater

When I was eleven or maybe twelve, I went to a performance at Proud Theater with some of my mom's friends. *Oh, yeah, it's so good,* I thought. When I turned thirteen, my mother's friend's son and I decided to check it out.

It was in a church, the sub-sub-basement of a church. We went down a flight of stairs, then another flight of stairs, then another flight of stairs, until we're basically in a fallout shelter.

Luke and his friend Samuel found themselves in a big room filled with a bunch of high-school seniors. It was a bit intimidating.

We were sitting by ourselves in a little corner 'cause everybody's, like, twice as tall as us, twice as old as us—well, not exactly. One guy, Seb, came up to us. He was wearing a skirt, and his hair was long. He said, "Hey, it's so great you came! You're like little children, and you're here and that's awesome. Like, high five!"

I was cool with that. "Yay, you accept me. At least you're being nice to me."

A twenty-year-old transgender playwright-mentor, who joined us for one

153

of our interviews, was at the rehearsal too. He actually helped the two young actors through a warm-up session that begins every rehearsal. The playwright explained that Luke did not talk to him at first.

Yep. For the first six months, I didn't talk to him.

"I used to be intimidating," the playwright says with a laugh.

And I used to be shy as hell. I would go to Proud Theater and talk to my friend Samuel. I would follow him around because he was less shy than I was. I'm shy even around people my age, and these people were three or four years older than me.

After maybe four or five months of silence, Emma, an adult mentor, got me out of my shell. Emma became my first friend in Proud Theater other than Samuel. I thought, *You can actually talk to these people.*

During my first year with the group, the playwright wrote a skit called "Do It Yourself." I got cast as the trans man. Even though I was still identifying as female, I remember trying out for the part and really wanting it. But I didn't actually know why.

"Do It Yourself" is like a foggy mirror, artfully hinting at the playwright's mind-set before he came out trans to his parents. He told me that he chose to give the lead to Luke because he saw a lot of his own earlier behavior in the young actor. "I thought it would be interesting to give him the role and see what he would do with it. I figured by playing it, maybe it could get the gender identity ball rolling. If nothing else, it would be a great role for him."

Scene ii: Third-Grade Bully

Probably the first major bully was in third grade. He made the usual generic insults for bullying trans people: "Are you a boy or a girl?" he would ask me. He asked a lot. "Are you a boy or a girl? Are you a boy or a girl? Do you want to be a boy?" I think he may have had a Napoleon complex because he was a small kid. He was athletic and good in sports, though.

154

I was good in sports too, but I didn't participate much. When we played, we were always separated by gender, and I felt really uncomfortable playing with the girls. When I did play with the boys, if I did something wrong, I'd be so mortified that I'd be too embarrassed to go back and play again. Oh, my gosh, I was, like, deathly, deathly shy.

Scene iii: Middle-School Bullies

When I got to middle school, it got a lot worse—especially in sixth grade. There was this guy who . . . oh, my God . . . who was very, very—he was one of those people who was the typical popular jock type. Big. Tall. Athletic. Handsome. Stuff like that. Yeah. He was definitely one of the main harassers. He had a couple of guys who would accompany him. It was mostly verbal. When you are questioning whether you *are* a boy or a girl, and someone comes right out and asks you, "Are you a boy or a girl?" it's like rubbing alcohol on a cut.

It only got physical a couple of times. I reported it once. The whole experience was so humiliating and useless that it kind of made me feel that I couldn't trust the school system. One guy was coming on with the usual are-you-a-guy-or-a-girl-do-you-want-to-be-a-boy stuff. It was one of the first weeks in middle school, so I thought, *You know, it's middle school. I should not take this anymore. I need to do something.* And I went to the teacher and said that I'd like to file a harassment report. As far as I know, the report wasn't filed. They had me go into a room with him and asked me to tell him why I was upset. And he had to say "sorry." It was very juvenile. It was very ineffective. A lot of it was mortifying because I didn't like talking about harassment. When I did, it tended to bring more attention to what I was harassed about, which was gender expression.

I came out as trans to my mom. We were in the kitchen, sitting at the table. I think it was after school, but I don't remember exactly. I was feeling emotionally shaky, and I don't remember how it came out, but it did.

She quickly denied it, saying, "I don't think you are."

My older sister was there. She told my mom that if I said I was, I probably was. She actually said that to my mom, which I really appreciated. But my mom still said, "No, I don't think you are." That cut pretty deep, deep enough that I dropped it.

I had a couple of journal entries around that time: *I guess I'm a boy . . . I'm a boy . . . I'm a boy.* After my mom denied it, I stopped writing about it. I stopped thinking about it. When I stopped talking about it, my sister stopped too.

Scene iv: Seventh-Grade Fem

In seventh grade, there were attempts by the girls to fem me up. A couple of times, they held me down and put makeup on my face. To them it was very, very funny. Part of me didn't want to say anything because, in a twisted sort of way, I was making people laugh. It was a chance to please people, so I didn't tell anyone. Besides, I called these girls my friends. You always want to be able to have somebody as your friend. No one wants to say I don't have any friends. And out of everybody in the school, they were the ones who paid me the most attention, so that translated into, oh, they're friends.

I didn't think I could tell my parents about them. I was afraid that Mom might have said what my friends did was for my own good. I mean, I don't think she'd really say that, but there was always the fear that she might. Part of that was because when I dressed more female-like, because all my male clothes were dirty or something, my mom would say, "Oh, you look so nice today." I didn't look especially nice. I just looked more female.

Scene v: Eighth-Grade Actor

I really, really enjoy acting. It's the one thing that I've had positive feedback about all my life. I acted in school plays, little things on campus, basically wherever I could. It's definitely a passion of mine. And it's one of the few things I like doing that I've been told I do well. That gave me the confidence to try out for the play.

I kept a folder with all my Proud Theater scripts in it. I printed out information about testosterone and stuff like that, telling myself I was doing all this research for the skit, that I wanted to know about being trans for the skit. It was a total lie.

Portraying a trans person came really, really easily. "Hmmm, this feels right. Maybe I am trans." I mean, in an oversimplified version of things, because I was acting the role of a trans man, I could explore being trans deeper than I could by just thinking about it. It was, like, "I'm not reading this stuff because I'm trans; I'm reading it because the character's trans." In reality it was a huge personal exploration.

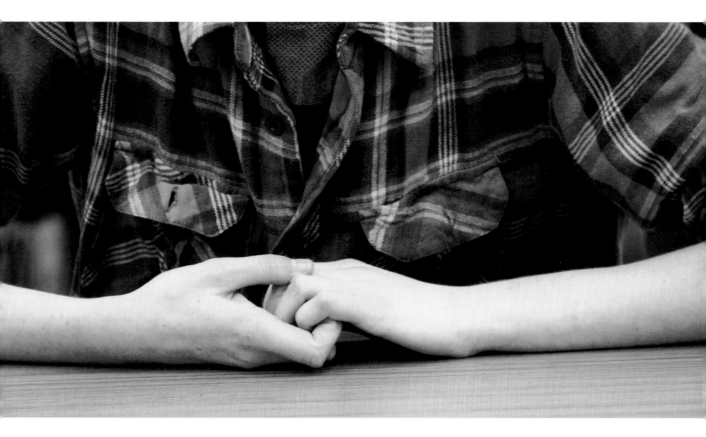

Acting is so strange. You become someone else. Their troubles are your troubles. So it gets blurry, especially in this case. Who is who? Who is what?

At the time, I still identified as gay. I never liked using the word lesbian because it implies female. If anyone ever asked me, I'd say I was gay, not lesbian. I was on the verge of questioning my gender when I was cast in the part. It kinda allowed me to question more.

During a rehearsal, the playwright came up to me and said, "So I heard you were questioning stuff. Do you want to talk about it?"

And I was, like, "*Yes!* That would be awesome!"

I could talk to Samuel, but I didn't really. The playwright became a role model for me. I had had role models in the past, but I always felt a sense of competition because they were male-bodied and I wasn't. With him it was like, "Whoa, this is a male person who isn't male-bodied, and I can really, really relate to you."

My family was okay with me being gay, but trans was a different issue for them. I think a lot of it was because they had no experience with it. My mom said, "I'm going to be an okay-onboard mom, and you're going to be a lesbian. I'm okay with that."

Scene vi: Summertime Love

Toward the end of eighth grade, Luke started dating.

So it was, "Stop everything. I have a girlfriend! Yay!"

I really, really liked this girl. She was cute, she was funny, she was intelligent, and all that stuff. She was someone I had known since sixth grade. We had always been grouped together because we were the quiet, intelligent people. It wasn't like a slick kind of friendship. We were incredibly awkward. She was even shyer than I was. She almost never said anything. And she would never talk about things that involved emotions. When I finally got up the nerve to tell her I liked her, her response was just, "Okay, I kinda figured."

Maybe a month later, I found out that she liked me too.

The awkwardness got even worse when we started dating. When I look back on it now, I clench up. It was very, very awkward. A lot of silences, stuff like that. But even so, I was totally elated. I thought about her the entire summer. It's hard to concentrate on being trans when you have a girlfriend.

By the end of summer, the couple broke up.

I felt it was just too awkward. It wasn't a bad breakup. It was, like, this is awkward and we should probably stop torturing ourselves.

Scene vii: Ninth Grade

Once the school year started, I was thinking about the trans thing again. It's weird. I was quite convinced I was trans in sixth grade, but because of my mom's reaction, I took her word for it that I wasn't. I put it from my mind.

I slowly started to rediscover my gender in eighth grade. So there were two separate processes—sixth grade and eighth grade—a double discovery process. When I came out to my mom this second time, we talked about my taking hormones because that was what I wanted to do.

I was a lot more nervous coming out to my dad than I was with my mom. My dad's generally less accepting, I guess.

Three years earlier, when I came out to him as gay, I had thought about how to do it a lot. I was really stressed about it, and I ended up deliberately coming out to him at the worst time. He was angry with my older sister, who had come home late and hadn't called, and the dinner was burned, and my sister was on the verge of tears, and he was yelling, and while all this stuff was happening, I said, "Hey, Dad, I'm gay!" I figured it couldn't get any worse so I should just say it. Everything got very quiet. He was just like, "Uh, okay." It got tense. It was tense before, and now it was very tense.

Personally I was a lot more relieved when I said it. Once you get over that initial hurdle of saying the words, "I'm 'fill-in-the-blank,'" it's generally easier. I don't remember too much about what happened afterward. I don't think there was a lot of talking, just tense silence. A couple of weeks later, he gave me a book by Ellen DeGeneres. He said, "Here's this book. She's a lesbian," and he walked away. It was a good book; she's a very funny lady.

A couple of weeks after coming out trans to my mom, I came out to my dad. He was dropping me and my older sister off at school; I got out of the car and was about to shut the door. . . .

"Dad, I'm trans."

"Well, okay."

"Okay, bye," and I shut the door and ran off.

We didn't really talk about it until a couple of days later. There was more explaining about what that meant. Everyone knows what gay is. Nobody knew what trans is.

I explained that "I'm mentally male and I would like it if you use male pronouns and stuff." He wasn't dubious like my mom was, but he didn't think it was . . . well . . . he thought it was a phase and was waiting for it to go away.

My parents were definitely worried about health issues. My mom especially was worried about health risks involved with taking hormones because she was unsure about the process.

At Luke's request, people started using male pronouns.

Some had more trouble than others. I didn't find it offensive because it was understandable. I was messed up in my head about it too. I'd screw up. I'd refer to myself, saying, "Oh, *she's* doing something about something." Wait a minute! I'm supposed to be using male pronouns. I identify as male now.

It took about a year to convince my mom to use male pronouns. My dad was pretty against it until a couple of months ago. My dad still calls my hormones steroids rather than T, which I asked him not to do. He messes up with pronouns a lot and doesn't apologize for it. He uses my birth name a lot. But I don't actually care. It's definitely better than before. Now everything was out in the open.

Scene viii: The Performance

The opportunity to go onstage kind of melded me together. I am definitely less shy now than I used to be. I try to keep some of the energy I have onstage offstage. I'm still most comfortable onstage.

The night Luke played the leading role in "Do It Yourself," he also performed a monologue that he wrote.

I remember standing backstage, about to go on with my monologue, being soooo, so scared. As soon as it ended, I was utterly, utterly elated. It's the best feeling to be onstage and do something you love and do it well.

Opening night was great. It was only topped by the night after, which was when my friends came. The house was sold out. It was a great audience.

In performance

They were laughing, crying all over the place. I remember feeling very proud to be doing that play before my friends. I was definitely introducing transgender to them.

It was thrilling, quite thrilling.

NOTES AND RESOURCES

AUTHOR'S NOTE

So here we are, a pack of *Homo sapiens* thinking that we know whether a person is female or male. Now that I've spent a few years researching and talking with people who fall under the transgender umbrella, I am confident saying that male/female is not the only way to describe gender. The people I've come to know and love in the course of writing and photographing this book have helped me better understand the fluidity of gender and sex.

This lesson for me also reinforces what I've been writing about for years: once we get to know individuals who may be different from ourselves, it is less likely we will be wary of them. And maybe, just maybe, we will learn a little more about ourselves.

Nuts and Bolts

The basic plan for *Beyond Magenta* was to write and photograph a narrative nonfiction book about sex and alienation, two universal themes that have interacted in life, literature, and art since forever. The focus was to explore basic characteristics of sexuality, especially watershed periods when young people recognize or begin to acknowledge their sexual and gender identities. The book was going to be about boys who realize that they are girls and girls who realize that they are boys. As you can see, this vision changed as I learned more.

A nonfiction author is nothing without facts and contacts. After reading books and attending conferences to understand basic issues facing the transgender community, I began the search for an organization that would help me find participants willing to reveal themselves in print and, sometimes, pictures.

Friend and law professor Susan Herman, usually my first contact for books about human or civil rights, put me in touch with James D. Esseks, the director of the ACLU's Lesbian, Gay, Bisexual, Transgender & AIDS Project. James, in turn, identified a number of organizations I might want to reach.

Eventually, I found the right, spot-on group. The Callen-Lorde Community

Health Center not only had a first-rate reputation, but it also had a specially designed teen program called Health Outreach to Teens, HOTT.

Trey Gantt, the program coordinator, and Reed Christian, the program director, arranged a staff meeting where I presented my proposal. Well, it was a little more complicated than that. CLCHC needed to be sure I was who I said I was, and that I was doing what I said I was doing. I appreciated their caution. It meant that they were respectful of their clients and professional in the way they go about their work. In the two years working with the HOTT staff, I was never, ever disappointed.

One of the therapists, Nicole Davis, became my go-to spokesperson. A compassionate psychologist and all-around amazing person, Nicole totally got what was needed to bring about as full a picture as possible about transgender teens. It was important to find youths from wide-ranging ethnic, religious, and socio-economic circles so as not to mislabel "transgender" as rich or poor, white or of color. Through Nicole, I met Jessy, Christina, Mariah, and Cameron.

Nicole, who was pregnant at the time, arranged for her colleague Amelie Davidson to take over our project once her child was born. Amelie introduced me to Nat and Dr. Manel Silva.

Process

The process of converting taped conversations into readable narratives is delicate. On the one hand, a person's voice and life need to be reported accurately. On the other hand, their story has to be revealed in an interesting, readable narrative. The profiles you read were taken from a series of taped interviews that were edited by me. When information on the tapes was not relevant to the narrative's topic, it was deleted. When information was not clear, I sought clarification from the participants. The participants were then invited to read their chapters. We worked together to make sure that everything written was honest and authentic.

All of the participants had the choice of whether or not to use their real names. They also had the option to include photographs. Jessy, Christina, Cameron, Nat, and I created individual photo essays to fit their chapters. For example, Nat and I called their essay, "The Long Road with Musical Interludes," and decided it would be best photographed in black and white.

As we worked, the tapes and e-mails, laughter and tears, trusts and convictions, transitioned into *Beyond Magenta.*

It became clear that *Beyond Magenta* needed to spread its wings and move to at least one other part of the country to expand the representation. That meant long-distance research. In situations such as this, my first call is either to a friend, a librarian, or a teacher.

Kathleen T. Horning, the director of the Cooperative Children's Book Center at the University of Wisconsin–Madison meets all three criteria. She was my first and only e-mail. I became Tom Sawyer as K.T. painted my literary fence. She researched, called, cajoled, and re-called people to find the perfect group for *Beyond Magenta.* Through K.T.'s friend Carin Bringelson, I met the marvelous folks at Proud Theater.

Callen Harty, Brian Wild, and Sol Kelley-Jones asked their teenage theater company if I could attend their closed rehearsals. Lucky for *Beyond Magenta,* lucky for me, they agreed. It was there I met Luke. I wish I could include every member of the company — they are a remarkably talented group of people. They are also an excellent example of how the artistic process can open a door to a deeper understanding of oneself, others, and social relationships.

K.T. and her partner, the writer Emily Kokie, not only housed and fed me — very well I might add — but also had a closing night "strike party" for Proud Theater principals. Two perks for writers of nonfiction are: we meet very interesting people and eat very good food.

Acknowledgments

Lots of people helped make this book possible. I owe them an enormous debt of gratitude.

First and forever, I am grateful to Jessy; Nan; Christina; Christina's mother, Wanda; Mariah; Cameron; Nat; and Luke for their insight, generosity, honesty, humor, and bravery.

Much appreciation goes to the participants' families who generously donated photographs from their family albums.

The Callen-Lorde staff, especially Nicole Davis, Amelie Davidson, Trey Gantt, Tia Pinkson-Burke, Reed Christian, and Jerry Algozer, were instrumental in making this book happen. Dr. Manel Silva, the clinical director of the

HOTT program, took time from her very busy practice to talk with me and review the medical sections of the book.

Callen Harty and Brian Wild were steadfast in their support, wise counsel, and friendship. Their commitment to the Proud Theater is gift to both performers and audience. A special thanks to Callen Harty for allowing the use of his sensitive photograph of Luke performing. Thanks to Luke and his family for their gracious permission to reproduce "Untouchable." I learn more every time I read it.

My prolific and fabulously talented writer friends, Robie Harris, Deborah Heiligman, and Elizabeth Levy, took time from their own work to read the manuscript. Their critiques were pitch-perfect. I can't begin to say how much I value their help and their friendship. More good friends and family, including Stacy Goldate, Thea Lurie, and Arthur Pinto, held my hand, or their phones, throughout this journey, offering much-appreciated advice and encouragement. Thanks to Reed Christian and Karlan Sick for reading late drafts. If mistakes remain after so august a group of readers, they are solely mine.

Thanks to Kathleen Anderson at the International Center of Photography for her expert advice while helping me print and prepare the digital images.

Kenneth Wright, agent extraordinaire, formerly at the Writer's House, was yet another critical reader. Throughout this project he was enthusiastic and encouraging. I felt safe knowing that Ken had my back. When Ken moved on to another position in publishing, Brianne Johnson stepped in, embraced *Beyond Magenta,* and has become one terrific agent. Thank you both.

It is an absolute pleasure working with my editor, Hilary Van Dusen. Even very early on, she and her colleagues at Candlewick Press were quick to send me articles and materials that might help in the research of the book. I am also fortunate that Hannah Mahoney, Miriam Newman, Matt Roeser, and Sherry Fatla worked on the creative and technical elements in the book. What a team!

Last but always, thanks to one more reader, my husband, Bailey, who enriches life's adventure — the high eureka moments, the low grumpy ones — with love, support, grace, humor, and, above all, patience.

ABOUT THE CALLEN-LORDE COMMUNITY HEALTH CENTER

The Callen-Lorde Community Health Center is named after two beloved activists. Michael Callen (1955–1993) was a singer and composer. In 1982, he was diagnosed with AIDS. He became an activist, making people aware of the growing health crisis. With Peter Allen, he composed the song "Love Don't Need a Reason," and he also founded the Flirtations, an LGBT a cappella singing group.

Audre Lorde (1934–1992), the daughter of Grenadian parents, grew up in Harlem. She was a poet and prose writer. Her book *The Cancer Journals,* published in 1980, narrated her experiences as a breast-cancer patient. She was also a librarian and educator who became a leader in the lesbian activists community. From 1991 until her death, she was New York State's Poet Laureate.

In its mission statement, the clinic states that the "Callen-Lorde Community Health Center provides sensitive, quality health care and related services primarily to New York's lesbian, gay, bisexual, and transgender communities—in all their diversity—regardless of ability to pay."

The HOTT program (Health Outreach to Teens) is a primary-care medical facility for young people between the ages of thirteen and twenty-four. It specializes in mental and medical health care, sexually transmitted infection screening, HIV care, and transgender care. Teens meet in a youth-only medical suite or in a medical van that travels to areas throughout New York City.

Amelie Davidson, one of the two social worker–therapists at HOTT, deals with the mental health part of the clinic, where people are seen for a variety of concerns, including depression, anxiety, relationship issues, social isolation, coping with a new diagnosis, and gender-related issues. Amelie says, "In terms of transgender care, our intention is to create a space where young people can come at any stage of their transition process, get correct information, and be cared for and feel safe."

A person must be eighteen or older to be given hormone shots at Callen-Lorde. Although younger teen clients are able to work with HOTT therapists, they are referred to various hospitals for their hormone shots.

Q & A WITH DR. MANEL SILVA, CLINICAL DIRECTOR OF THE HOTT PROGRAM

Susan Kuklin: When is a person considered transgender?

Manel Silva: That depends on the person. Actually, it's one of the debates in the medical and political field: What does it mean to transition? For some people, it can be as simple as having other people acknowledge their gender identity and potentially their name change. For other people, it can be the full nine yards — hormone therapy, sexual reassignment, and other types of surgery.

SK: What causes a person to be transgender?

MS: I think the question should be flipped around: What's the cause for assuming that one's gender identity has to be the one that you are born with? When I first came into this job, I was much more comfortable about people's sexuality than I was with people's gender identity. But when you hear the same stories over and over again, from people from all over the world, you start realizing that transgender is not an anomaly. It's a part of the spectrum of people's realities. Then you stop wondering about the cause and you start realizing it's a part of reality.

SK: A person arrives at the clinic and says, "I know I want to transition, but I'm not sure how far I want to go." What's the process?

MS: At this clinic the first session is dedicated to figuring out what transitioning means to them. Often questioning gender identity begins way before they start to think about transitioning. They may not know that transition is an option. We ask how they learned about transitioning. What have they already done? What are they interested in doing?

By the time they've come here, though, most of the kids have already done a lot of research. They don't show up at a doctor's office on a whim, especially an eighteen-year-old, especially here. Many have been dressing as their preferred gender for several years. They've figured out what their support system is. They've generated the courage to out themselves just by coming here.

SK: Then what do you talk about?

MS: Basic things: relationships, food, shelter, money, and education. How are other people going to deal with your transition? Will your family accept you? Will they let you stay in the house? If they kick you out, where are you going to go? Do you feel comfortable transitioning in your job? Or do you feel you have to take time off? How are you going to support yourself at that time? The same questions are true about school.

SK: What are the social risks?

MS: A lot of the risks in transitioning have less to do with hormones or surgeries than with how society deals with folks who are transgender. It's about how you out yourself. It's really about how society deals with people who are transgender, and the very real experience of transphobia. For example, when it comes to dating, you might find yourself in a dangerous situation. Or if your parents find out, you may get kicked out of the house. Being transgender and wanting to transition is often a very marginalizing experience because of the lack of acceptance in society.

This is also the reason why, as a clinic, we've decided to provide hormones and medical care for free to all our teen patients. We feel that removing as many barriers as possible allows these young people to engage with us on a regular basis. We get to help them mitigate those risks and support them in their life decisions. Intervening before they become homeless or before they get in other risky situations prevents a lot of negative consequences and enables them to live their lives fully.

SK: What about the medical risks of hormones?

MS: Let me start by saying that cancer is not one of the known main risks. Everybody thinks it is, but it's not. There are risks like blood clots, especially if you smoke. High blood pressure can be a risk. It can increase the risk of heart attack and stroke over the long run. These are not minor things. But they can be monitored clinically. We measure cholesterol levels. We do liver-function tests.

These risks are the reasons we encourage people to go through their transition in a monitored environment. We're not going to just give people hormones and never see them again. I tell folks, "You can always get hormones off the street. You know that because that's what some of your friends do. But the reason it's important to get hormones here is we can monitor you."

A big issue is the emotional impact hormones can have on people. Adding hormones to your body is not a benign psychological process. That's another reason we encourage people, particularly in the beginning, to be engaged in therapy. It is emotionally discombobulating when you start hormones. You might feel a little bit more aggressive than you did before starting testosterone. If you've had a hard time managing aggression in the past or you live in an abusive household, that's where risk can come in.

SK: What role do genes play?

MS: This is another part of the spectrum, especially where intersex people fit into the transgender model. There's definite overlap there. Folks who are born intersex have ambiguous genitalia because of genetic predeterminants. For example, someone who has an extra X or extra Y chromosome may have genitalia that don't look stereotypically male or female. So they don't fit into society's version of bio-male and bio-female. In fact, historically society has forced people to undergo sexual assignment surgery at very young ages, even when they are first born. That's our need to have people fit into our gender role models. For the vast majority of gender nonconforming people, their intrinsic identity is not determined by genetics. At HOTT, we place heavy value on the patient's self-identity.

SK: What kind of exams do you do?

MS: During the first two visits, we do the lab work, such as blood and urine analysis, to get a baseline and to make sure nothing drastic is going on. We do a physical exam, but if someone declines a physical exam, that's not a reason to refuse them hormones.

SK: What else does the clinic provide?

MS: Transitioning is not just about hormones. For example, we talk about the medical effects of binding, making sure they are tucking properly. I had someone come in the other day who was using an Ace bandage to bind his breasts. An Ace bandage is equally binding front and back, whereas a binder has more leeway in the back so you can breathe. You are less likely to pass out. The Ace bandage limits your lungs.

We also provide legal referrals to help with name and identity changes.

SK: What about recreational drugs or drinking?

MS: We talk about the side effects of drugs or alcohol. We try to move them to deal with addiction. We support them in any way we can.

SK: Can you give a person hormone therapy while they are dealing with overcoming addiction?

MS: Sure. There are rare contraindications. There's no medical interaction between most common drugs and hormones. It's not a good idea to drink when you're taking estrogen, for example, because your liver metabolizes estrogen. But unless you have actual liver damage, it's not that problematic.

If a person's suicidal, we worry that hormones could increase that. But half the time, the reason trans folks are suicidal is because they can't access hormone therapy. By withdrawing hormones, you can actually precipitate someone feeling suicidal. So you have to be able to differentiate those two things. This is why we do a really good history on somebody.

SK: What happens when a person gets their first hormone shot? Is it scary? Is it exciting?

MS: Oh, my God, they're so excited about it. There's rarely anything that a clinic can do for a teenager that makes them so excited. Normally, two exciting things are curing an STD or a negative pregnancy test. This tops it all. It's life changing, and it's life affirming. This is what they've been waiting for their whole lives. It's a privilege to be part of that process.

To learn more about the Callen-Lorde Community Health Center, visit their website at http://callen-lorde.org.

ABOUT PROUD THEATER

In 1999, thirteen-year-old Sol Kelley-Jones picked up the phone and called Callen Harty, forty-three. Callen was an established actor and playwright at the Broom Street Theater in Madison, Wisconsin. Although they had heard about each other because they were both advocates for gay rights, they had never met. Sol, the daughter of lesbian parents, was interested in theater, politics, and activism. Sol asked Callen to help her start a theater group for gay and lesbian youth. Callen said yes.

The first year, only three gay teenagers signed on. (Currently there are thirty teen actors.) They had no funding. Churches around town gave them free rehearsal space. A few years into the program, some of the adults involved put up money to rent the main theater on the University of Wisconsin campus. They sold out the show and from that point on were able to pay their own way.

Proud Theater is a nonprofit, all-volunteer organization that is composed of LGBT youth, allies, and children of LGBT parents. Sol describes their work as "a belief in the power of art to create change. The process of creating artwork out of youths' experiences is radical, is transforming, and is healing. It is also healing to communities. It can have profound ripples.

"We consider ourselves an activist organization, an artistic organization, and also a youth-development organization. We're developing leaders, stories, and strategies about how to use art to create new realities. Not only do we reflect on some of the horrors and some of the oppression that young people have faced—homophobia, heterosexism, transphobia, and racism—but we also look at the joy and the celebration of different identities. We look at what we want the world to be like. I think theater is a magical place where you can experiment with what isn't yet."

Proud Theater is often invited by churches, AIDS networks, senior centers, and schools to perform their plays. The company is expanding. They recently started Proud Theater–Wausau. Wausau is a small, conservative city, yet ten kids show up each week.

Callen says, "Proud Theater has become a lifeline to them. That's what we're most proud of."

To learn more about Proud Theater, visit their website at http://www.proud theater.org.

GLOSSARY

androgen: a male sex hormone, such as testosterone

androgynous: refers to a combination of masculine and feminine, often in appearance

down-low: a man who identifies as heterosexual but has sex with men

dysphoric: a state of unease or dissatisfaction with life

estrogen: a steroid hormone that is the primary female sex hormone; it promotes the development of female characteristics of the body

FTM (female to male): a person assigned female at birth but who identifies as male; a trans man

homophobic: having an extreme revulsion to homosexuals and homosexuality

hormone: a chemical released by a cell or a gland that affects cells in other parts of the body

intersex: a genetic condition in which a person is born with external genitalia and internal sex organs that are in between typically male and typically female

metrosexual: a male with a strong aesthetic sense who spends a great deal of effort on his appearance and lifestyle

mindfulness: a heightened consciousness or awareness of something or someone else

MTF (male to female): a person assigned male at birth but who identifies as female; a trans woman

neuron: a nerve cell that processes and transmits information by electrical and chemical signaling

pansexual: having a sexual preference that is not limited by gender identity or sexual orientation

placement: refers to residential treatment centers or facilities

pound: slang for a manly greeting

synapse: a place or junction between two cells where a nerve impulse is transmitted from one neuron to another

testes: components of the reproductive and endocrine systems in male-bodied people; their primary function is to produce sperm and androgens, mostly testosterone

testosterone: a steroid hormone that plays a key role in the development of male reproductive tissues, testes, and prostate, as well as secondary sexual characteristics such as increased muscle, bone mass, and body hair

transgender: a general term that refers to a person whose gender identity, expression, or behavior does not conform to that typically associated with the sex to which they were assigned at birth

transphobia: having an extreme revulsion to transgender people

RESOURCES

Books

NONFICTION

Bailey, J. Michael. *The Man Who Would Be Queen: The Science of Gender-Bending and Transsexualism*. Washington, DC: Joseph Henry Press, 2003.

Bornstein, Kate. *Gender Outlaw: On Men, Women, and the Rest of Us*. New York: Vintage, 1995.

——, and S. Bear Bergman. *Gender Outlaws: The Next Generation*. Berkeley, CA: Seal Press, 2010.

Boylan, Jennifer Finney. *She's Not There: A Life in Two Genders*. New York: Broadway Books, 2003.

Brill, Stephanie, and Rachel Pepper. *The Transgender Child: A Handbook for Families and Professionals*. San Francisco: Cleis Press, 2008.

Green, Jamison. *Becoming a Visible Man*. Nashville, TN: Vanderbilt University Press, 2004.

Herman, Joanne. *Transgender Explained: For Those Who Are Not*. Bloomington, IN: Author House, 2009.

Mattilda, a.k.a. Matt Bernstein Sycamore. *Nobody Passes: Rejecting the Rules of Gender and Conformity*. Berkeley, CA: Seal Press, 2006.

Sinnott, Megan J. *Toms and Dees: Transgender Identity and Female Same-Sex Relationships in Thailand*. Honolulu: University of Hawaii Press, 2004.

Stryker, Susan. *Transgender History*. Berkeley, CA: Seal Press, 2008.

FICTION

Eugenides, Jeffrey. *Middlesex*. New York: Farrar, Straus & Giroux, 2002.

Peters, Julie Anne. *Luna*. New York: Little, Brown, 2004.

Movies

The Adventures of Priscilla, Queen of the Desert (Poly Gram, 1994)

Boys Don't Cry (Fox Searchlight, 1999)

The Crying Game (Palace Pictures, 1992)

Hedwig and the Angry Inch (Killer Films/New Line Cinema, 2001)

M. Butterfly (Geffen Pictures/Miranda Productions, 1993)

Transamerica (Belladonna Productions, 2005)

Service and Advocacy Organizations

Here are a few of the many organizations where transgender youth and their families and friends can get help, information, and support.

The Callen-Lorde Community Health Center is the health center featured in this book. http://callen-lorde.org

The Door is a youth program in New York City that offers support, legal services, GED resources, referrals, and health services, including a wide range of programs and services geared toward LGBTQ youth. http://www.door.org

The Gay-Straight Alliance Network empowers youth activists to fight homophobia and transphobia in schools. http://gsanetwork.org

Gender Spectrum provides education, training, and support to help create a gender sensitive and inclusive environment for all children and teens. http://www.genderspectrum.org

Intersex Initiative is a Portland, Oregon, based national activist and advocacy organization for people born with intersex conditions. It was founded by Emi Koyama, a multi-issue social-justice activist and former intern at the Intersex Society of North America. http://www.intersexinitiative.org

The Intersex Society of North America is devoted to systemic change to end shame, secrecy, and unwanted genital surgeries for people born with an anatomy that someone decided is not standard for male or female. http://www.isna.org

It Gets Better is a video project that spreads the message of hope for LGBTQ teens. http://www.itgetsbetter.org

Parents, Families and Friends of Lesbians and Gays (PFLAG) is a national organization that promotes the health and well-being of lesbian, gay, bisexual, and transgender persons, as well as their families and friends. http://community.pflag.org

Proud Theater is the LGBTQ teen theater group featured in this book. http://www.proudtheater.org

Trans Youth Family Allies empowers children and families by partnering with educators, service providers, and communities to develop supportive environments in which gender may be expressed and respected. http://www.imatyfa.org

The Trevor Project is an organization that provides crisis intervention and suicide prevention services to LGBTQ youth. http://www.thetrevorproject.org

Legal Organizations

The American Civil Liberties Union (ACLU) includes among its missions the championing of the rights of transgender people to live their lives freely and

with respect: "We fight for protections against discrimination in employment, housing, public accommodations (including schools), and health care. We also challenge obstacles to people obtaining government identity documents respectful of their gender identity, as well as barriers to transgender parents seeking continuing relationships with their children."
http://www.aclu.org/lgbt-rights/discrimination-against-transgender-people

Lambda Legal is a national organization committed to achieving full recognition of the civil rights of lesbians, gay men, bisexuals, transgender people, and those with HIV through impact litigation, education, and public-policy work. http://www.lambdalegal.org

The National Center for Transgender Equality is a national social-justice organization dedicated to advancing the equality of transgender people through advocacy, collaboration, and empowerment. http://transequality.org

The Peter Cicchino Youth Project at the Urban Justice Center reaches out to LGBT and straight teenagers living on the streets of New York City. http://www.urbanjustice.org/ujc/projects/peter.html

The Sylvia Rivera Law Project works to guarantee that all people are free to self-determine gender identity and expression, regardless of income or race, and without facing harassment, discrimination, or violence. http://srlp.org

The Transgender Law Center works to change law, policy, and attitudes so that all people can live safely, authentically, and free from discrimination regardless of their gender identity or expression. http://transgenderlawcenter.org

The Transgender Legal Defense & Education Fund is committed to ending discrimination based on gender identity and expression and to achieving equality for transgender people through public education, test-case litigation, direct legal services, community organizing, and public-policy efforts. http://www.transgenderlegal.org

As I learn of more organizations for transgender youths, I will post them on my website: www.susankuklin.com.